SOCIAL JUSTICE, EQUALITY AND EMPOWERMENT

THE LEGALIZATION OF SAME-SEX MARRIAGE

BACKGROUND AND FINAL RULING

SOCIAL JUSTICE, EQUALITY AND EMPOWERMENT

Additional books in this series can be found on Nova's website under the Series tab.

Additional e-books in this series can be found on Nova's website under the e-book tab.

SOCIAL JUSTICE, EQUALITY AND EMPOWERMENT

THE LEGALIZATION OF SAME-SEX MARRIAGE

BACKGROUND AND FINAL RULING

KENDRA VASQUEZ
EDITOR

nova publishers
New York

Library of Congress Cataloging-in-Publication Data

ISBN: 978-1-63483-942-6

Published by Nova Science Publishers, Inc. † New York

CONTENTS

PREFACE

The issue of same-sex marriage generates debate on both the federal and state levels. Either legislatively or judicially, same-sex marriage is legal in more than a dozen states. Conversely, many states have statutes and/or constitutional amendments limiting marriage to the union of one man and one woman. These state-level variations raise questions about the validity of such unions outside the contracted jurisdiction and have bearing on the distribution of state and/or federal benefits. As federal agencies grappled with the interplay of the Defense of Marriage Act (DOMA) and the distribution of federal marriage-based benefits, questions arose regarding DOMA's constitutionality and the appropriate standard (strict, intermediate, or rational basis) of review to apply to the statute. In *United States v. Windsor*, the U.S. Supreme Court struck down the federal ban on benefits for legally married same-sex couples. However, the Court indicated that it was taking no position on a state's authority to forbid same-sex marriages. Lower courts have interpreted *Windsor* broadly and have found such bans to violate equal protection and due process principles. This book provides a legal background after *United States v. Windsor*. The book provides background on, and analysis of, significant legal issues surrounding the same-sex marriage debate. It provides background on the constitutional principles that are often invoked in attempting to invalidate same-sex marriage bans—namely, equal protection and due process guarantees. It discusses key cases that led to the existing circuit split on the constitutionality of state same-sex marriage bans. Finally, this book explains the central issues in the circuit split and analyzes how the Supreme Court might resolve them on appeal.

In: The Legalization of Same-Sex Marriage
Editor: Kendra Vasquez
ISBN: 978-1-63483-942-6

Chapter 1

SAME-SEX MARRIAGE: A LEGAL BACKGROUND AFTER *UNITED STATES V. WINDSOR*[*]

Alison M. Smith

SUMMARY

The issue of same-sex marriage generates debate on both the federal and state levels. Either legislatively or judicially, same-sex marriage is legal in more than a dozen states. Conversely, many states have statutes and/or constitutional amendments limiting marriage to the union of one man and one woman. These state-level variations raise questions about the validity of such unions outside the contracted jurisdiction and have bearing on the distribution of state and/or federal benefits. As federal agencies grappled with the interplay of the Defense of Marriage Act (DOMA) and the distribution of federal marriage-based benefits, questions arose regarding DOMA's constitutionality and the appropriate standard (strict, intermediate, or rational basis) of review to apply to the statute.

In *United States v. Windsor*, a closely divided U.S. Supreme Court held that Section 3 of DOMA, which prohibited federal recognition of same-sex marriage, violated due process and equal protection

[*] This is an edited, reformatted and augmented version of a Congressional Research Service publication R43481, prepared for Members and Committees of Congress, dated October 10, 2014.

principles. As such, federal statutes that refer to a marriage and/or spouse for federal purposes should be interpreted as applying equally to legally married same-sex couples recognized by the state. However, the Court left unanswered questions such as (1) whether same-sex couples have a fundamental right to marry and (2) whether state bans on same-sex marriage are constitutionally permissible.

In the aftermath of the *Windsor* decision, lower federal courts have begun to address the constitutionality of state statutory and constitutional bans on same-sex marriage. To date, appellate courts in the Fourth, Seventh, Ninth and Tenth Circuits have upheld lower courts' decisions striking down such bans. The Fourth and Tenth Circuit Courts have concluded that the bans in three states (Utah, Oklahoma, and Virginia) violate both the equal protection and due process guarantees of the Fourteenth Amendment by impermissibly infringing on the fundamental right to marry. Relying on a series of "marriage" cases, these courts have taken a broad or expansive view of the fundamental right to marry and found that this right encompasses same-sex marriage and the recognition of these unions across state lines. While district courts were split as to the appropriate level of judicial review, both appellate courts concluded that strict scrutiny is appropriate as a fundamental right is implicated.

Although arriving at the same result as its sister circuits—striking down same-sex marriage bans (Indiana, Wisconsin, Idaho and Nevada)—the Seventh and Ninth Circuits took a different approach. They declined to address the issue of whether the fundamental right to marry encompasses same-sex unions. Instead, they limited their analysis to the equal protection challenge. The courts concluded that discrimination based on sexual orientation warrants heightened scrutiny and that the states' proffered justifications failed to further any legitimate purpose.

Appeals are pending in other circuits. The Sixth Circuit held oral arguments concerning the constitutionality of four states' (Kentucky, Michigan, Ohio, and Tennessee) bans. Some commentators believe that there is a possibility that the Sixth Circuit may uphold one or more of these bans. Recently, the Supreme Court denied review of petitions from the Fourth, Seventh, and Tenth Circuits (covering Indiana, Oklahoma, Utah, Virginia, and Wisconsin). It remains uncertain whether the U.S. Supreme Court will decline to intervene until a circuit split occurs.

INTRODUCTION

The recognition of same-sex marriage generates debate on both the federal and state levels. Either legislatively or judicially, same-sex marriage is legal in more than a dozen states and the District of Columbia.[1] Conversely, many states have statutory[2] or constitutional prohibitions[3] against same-sex marriage. Courts are beginning to address the constitutionality of these "defense of marriage" laws using equal protection and due process analysis. In *United States v. Windsor*,[4] the U.S. Supreme Court struck down the federal ban on benefits for legally married same-sex couples. However, the Court indicated that it was taking no position on a state's authority to forbid same-sex marriages. Lower courts have interpreted *Windsor* broadly and have found such bans to violate equal protection and due process principles.

GENERAL CONSTITUTIONAL PRINCIPLES

Equal Protection[5]

The Fourteenth Amendment provides, in relevant part, that "[n]o State shall ... deny to any person within its jurisdiction the equal protection of the laws."[6] Under the Supreme Court's equal protection jurisprudence, "the general rule is that legislation is presumed to be valid and will be sustained if the classification drawn by the statute is rationally related to a legitimate state interest."[7] Laws based on suspect classifications such as race or gender, however, typically receive heightened scrutiny and require a stronger, if not compelling, state interest to justify the classification.

Traditionally, courts have not considered sexual orientation to be a suspect category. In theory, therefore, the government need only advance a rational basis for enacting a statute that treats individuals differently depending on their sexual orientation. However, Supreme Court and recent lower court rulings have raised questions about whether classifications involving sexual orientation can meet this most deferential standard of review.

For example, in *Romer v. Evans*, the Court held that Amendment 2 of the Colorado constitution, which barred localities from enacting civil rights protections on the basis of sexual orientation, violated the Equal Protection Clause.[8] According to the Court, the Colorado amendment violated the guarantee of equal protection because the law was motivated strictly by animus and because there was otherwise no rational basis for enacting such a sweeping restriction on the legal rights of gays and lesbians.[9]

Substantive due Process (Right to Privacy)

The Fourteenth Amendment's Due Process Clause has a substantive component which "provides heightened protection against government interference with certain fundamental rights and liberty interests."[10] Although the Constitution does not specifically mention a fundamental right to privacy, courts recognize this right to encompass interpersonal relations.[11] For example, in *Lawrence v. Texas*,[12] the Court considered a constitutional challenge to a Texas statute that made it a crime for individuals to engage in homosexual sodomy. The Court held that the Fourteenth Amendment's due process privacy protections encompass private, consensual gay sex.[13]

While states have the authority to regulate marriage, this authority is not without limits. In a series of cases, the Court has struck down laws that impermissibly burden an individual's ability to exercise the right to marry.[14] For example, in *Loving v. Virginia*[15] the Court found that Virginia's anti-miscegenation statute violated both the Equal Protection Clause and Due Process Clause of the Fourteenth Amendment. The Court held that individuals could not be restricted from exercising their existing right to marry on account of the race of their chosen partner.[16] According to the Court,

> Marriage is one of the "basic civil rights of man," fundamental to our very existence and survival ... To deny this fundamental freedom on so unsupportable a basis as the racial classifications embodied in these statutes, classifications so directly subversive of the principle of equality at the heart of the Fourteenth Amendment, is surely to deprive all the State's citizens of liberty without due process of law. The Fourteenth Amendment requires that the freedom of choice to marry may not be restricted by invidious racial discrimination. Under our Constitution, the freedom to marry, or not marry, a person of another race resides with the individual and cannot be infringed by the State.

United States v. Windsor: The Challenge to the Federal Defense of Marriage Act

In *United States v. Windsor*,[17] a closely divided Court struck down a portion of the federal Defense of Marriage Act (DOMA),[18] finding that it violated the equal protection guarantees of the Fifth Amendment. DOMA was enacted "[t]o define and protect the institution of marriage." Section 2[19] allows all states, territories, possessions, and Indian tribes to refuse to recognize an act of any other jurisdiction that designates a relationship between individuals of the same sex as a marriage.[20] Section 3 had required that, for purposes of federal enactments, marriage would be defined as the union of one man and one woman.[21] As federal agencies grappled with the interplay of DOMA and the distribution of federal marriage-based benefits, questions arose regarding DOMA's constitutionality and the appropriate standard (strict, intermediate, or rational basis) of review to be applied to the statute.

In *Windsor*, the plaintiff and her late spouse were New York residents who had been legally married in Canada and whose same-sex marriage was legally recognized in New York. Because of DOMA, the decedent's estate could not claim the unlimited marital deduction for purposes of the federal estate tax. As a result, the estate owed $363,053 in taxes, which were paid. Ms. Windsor sued, claiming that Section 3 of DOMA violated the equal protection clause of the U.S. Constitution. Using a deferential rational basis review and ordering a refund of the taxes paid, the district court granted the plaintiff's motion for summary judgment holding that DOMA's definitional section was unconstitutional.[22] The lower court's ruling was affirmed on appeal; however, the appellate court determined that intermediate scrutiny was the appropriate level of review to apply to the provision.

In an opinion authored by Justice Kennedy, the Supreme Court relied on federalism, due process, and equal protection principles. The Court declined to determine whether Section 3 of DOMA is an unconstitutional "intrusion on state power." Instead the Court struck down the section on equal protection grounds using a "closer examination" and rational basis analysis.

In its opinion, the Court examined the historical relationship between the federal and state governments concerning domestic relations. Traditionally, states have maintained exclusive control over defining and regulating marriage. While marriage laws may vary among the states, marriages within a state are treated equally. According to the Court, Section 3 of DOMA runs contrary to this practice. Specifically, the Court noted that "[b]y creating two contradictory marriage regimes within the same State, DOMA forces same-sex couples to live as married for the purpose of state law but unmarried for the purpose of federal law, thus diminishing the stability and predictability of basic personal relations the State has found it proper to acknowledge and protect."[23]

After examining DOMA's history, the Court concluded that "its purpose is to discourage enactment of state same-sex marriage laws and to restrict the freedom and choice of couples married ... "[24] As such, the Court found Section

3 invalid, specifically stating that "no legitimate purpose overcomes the purpose and effect to disparage and to injure those whom the State, by its marriage laws, sought to protect in personhood and dignity."[25]

In their respective dissents, Chief Justice Roberts emphasized that the majority opinion only applied to actual marriages;[26] Justice Scalia speculated that the decision would lead to a constitutional right to same-sex marriage;[27] and Justice Alito argued that there is no constitutional right for same-sex couples to marry.[28]

While the Court resolved the question of the constitutionality of a federal definition of marriage excluding same-sex couples, it left unresolved several questions: (1) whether same-sex couples have a fundamental right to marry; (2) whether sexual orientation classifications warrant heightened scrutiny or the more deferential rational basis standard of review; (3) whether a state may prohibit same-sex marriages within its borders; and (4) whether a state may refuse to recognize a same-sex marriage validly contracted outside its borders.

POST-*WINDSOR* LITIGATION

In the aftermath of the *Windsor* decision, lower federal courts have begun to address the constitutionality of state statutory and constitutional bans on same-sex marriage and recognition of such unions.[29] To date, federal appellate courts in the Fourth,[30] Seventh,[31] and Tenth[32] Circuits as well as several federal district courts[33] have broadly construed *Windsor* and struck down state provisions which prohibit same-sex marriages within their borders. In *Kitchen v. Herbert*,[34] *Bishop v. Smith*,[35] and *Bostic v. Schaefer*,[36] both appellate courts affirmed lower court decisions which found that such bans violate both the equal protection and due process guarantees of the Fourteenth Amendment as they impermissibly infringe on the fundamental right to marry. In *Kitchen*, the court concluded that "a state may not deny the issuance of a marriage license to two persons, or refuse to recognize their marriage, based solely upon the sex of the persons in the marriage union."[37] Relying on a series of "marriage" cases, the appellate courts have taken an expansive view of the fundamental right to marry and found that the right encompasses same-sex unions and the recognition of these unions. While most district courts have used a rational basis review, both appellate courts concluded that strict scrutiny is appropriate as a fundamental right is implicated. Conversely, a federal district court upheld Louisiana's prohibition and nonrecognition of same-sex marriage against equal protection and due process challenges. [38]

According to the appellate courts, the fundamental right to marry includes the right to choose a same-sex partner and have that union recognized across state lines.[39] The courts relied on a series of cases in which the Supreme Court struck down laws that prohibited interracial marriage,[40] marriage of individuals owing child support,[41] and marriage of prison inmates.[42] Both circuit courts have determined that these cases demonstrate a broad right to marry "not circumscribed based on the characteristics of the individuals seeking to exercise that right."[43] The courts noted that the *Loving* Court did not create a new right to interracial marriage, but instead considered it to be a subset of "marriage." Accordingly, it follows that same-sex marriage is similarly included within the fundamental right to marry. According to the Fourth Circuit, these cases support the notion that the right to marry is a matter of an individual's freedom of choice.[44]

Both appellate courts applied strict scrutiny as the standard of review for equal protection and due process analysis, which requires the state to demonstrate that its classification is narrowly tailored to serve a compelling interest.[45] The states advanced several justifications including responsible procreation, optimal child-rearing, and civil strife. The courts rejected the states' justifications as they were mostly predicated on a link between marriage and procreation.[46] In essence, the court found the bans under inclusive as procreation is not a prerequisite to marriage for opposite-sex couples. As to the "civic strife" justification, the court in *Kitchen* noted that Supreme Court precedent has "repeatedly held that public opposition cannot provide cover for a violation of fundamental rights."[47] For these reasons, the appellate courts found that the bans violated both the equal protection and due process guarantees of the Fourteenth Amendment.

While the Seventh Circuit also struck down same-sex marriage bans before it in *Baskin v. Bogan*,[48] it took a different approach. The court declined to address the due process challenge and whether the fundamental right to marry encompasses same-sex unions. Instead, it focused on the equal protection challenge. In determining the appropriate level of review, the court found that "homosexuals are among the most stigmatized, misunderstood, and discriminated against minorities...."[49] Therefore, the court concluded that those individuals who seek to enter into a same-sex marriage are part of a quasi-suspect class requiring the government to advance a sufficiently persuasive justification for discrimination. The court found unpersuasive the proffered reasons for the bans: child welfare, preservation of traditional marriage, and procreation.[50] Moreover, the court noted that the "discrimination against same-sex couples is irrational, and therefore unconstitutional even if the discrimination is not subjected to heightened scrutiny...."[51]

IMPLICATIONS

A state's recognition of same-sex marriage implicates a myriad of benefits, rights, and responsibilities on both the federal and state levels. For example, for federal programs under the Social Security Administration's (SSA's) purview (Social Security, Medicare, and Supplemental Security Income), the agency generally defers to a state's definition of marriage. SSA guidance now allows for the payment of Social Security spousal benefits when the number holder (1) was married in a state that permits same-sex marriage; and (2) is domiciled (at the time of application, or while the claim is pending a final determination) in a state that recognizes same-sex marriage. On the state level, there may be tax implications as same-sex couples would be able to file a joint state tax return to match their federal return,[52] as well as implications for the holding, transfer, and inheritance of property.

CONCLUSION

The Supreme Court has not expressly resolved the issue of the constitutionality of state prohibitions or non-recognition of same-sex marriages. However, rulings in *Loving*, *Romer*, *Lawrence*, and *Windsor* appear to call into question the constitutionality of such prohibitions. Collectively, these cases prohibit states from passing laws based on animus toward gays and lesbians, extend constitutional protection to sexual choices of homosexuals, and prohibit the federal government from treating opposite-sex and same-sex marriages differently. Lower federal courts that have addressed the issue of state prohibitions on same-sex marriage have unanimously concluded that such bans violate equal protection and due process principles. While these courts recognize a state's power to regulate marriage, such regulation must comport with an individual's constitutional rights. These courts have rejected states' asserted governmental interests and instead found them not rationally related to the states' prohibitions of same-sex marriage. Two appellate courts have broadly interpreted the fundamental right to marriage to encompass same-sex marriages and the recognition of such unions. These courts concluded that the right to marry is a matter of an individual's freedom of choice. Rulings requiring states to recognize same-sex marriages entered in other states would apparently supercede and call into question the validity of Section 2 of DOMA, which permits the non-recognition of such unions. Additional rulings from the courts, including the Supreme Court, may be forthcoming before the validity of these state bans is definitively resolved.

End Notes

[1] California, Connecticut, Colorado, Delaware, Hawaii, Illinois, Iowa, Maine, Maryland, Massachusetts, Minnesota, New Hampshire, New Jersey, New Mexico, New York, Rhode Island, Vermont, and Washington.

[2] Indiana, Pennsylvania, West Virginia, and Wyoming.

[3] Alabama, Alaska, Arizona, Arkansas, Colorado, Florida, Georgia, Idaho, Kansas, Kentucky, Louisiana, Michigan, Missouri, Montana, Nebraska, Nevada, North Carolina, North Dakota, Ohio, Oklahoma, Oregon, South Carolina, South Dakota, Tennessee, Texas, Utah, Virginia, and Wisconsin.

[4] 133 S.Ct. 2675 (2013).

[5] The Fifth Amendment applies to the federal government while the Fourteenth Amendment applies to the states. In Bolling v. Sharpe (347 U.S. 497 [1954]), the Supreme Court interpreted the Fifth Amendment's Due Process Clause to include an equal protection element. In Buckley v. Valeo (424 U.S. 1, 93 [1976]), the Court stated that "[e]qual protection analysis in the Fifth Amendment area, is the same as that under the Fourteenth Amendment."

[6] U.S. Const. amend. XIV, §1.

[7] City of Cleburne v. Cleburne Living Center, 473 U.S. 432, 440 (1985).

[8] 517 U.S. 620, 635 (1996).

[9] Id. at 634.

[10] Washington v. Glucksberg, 521 U.S. 702, 720 (1997).

[11] Loving v. Virginia, 338 U.S. 1 (1967). In addition to the freedoms explicitly protected by the Bill of Rights, the "liberty" specifically protected by the Due Process Clause includes the right to have children, Skinner v. Oklahoma ex rel. Williamson, 316 U.S. 535 (1942); to direct the education and upbringing of one's children, Meyer v. Nebraska, 262 U.S. 390 (1923); Pierce v. Society of Sisters, 268 U.S. 510 (1925); to marital privacy, Griswold v. Connecticut, 381 U.S. 479 (1965); to use contraception, id.; Eisenstadt v. Baird, 405 U.S. 438 (1972); to bodily integrity, Rochin v. California, 342 U.S. 165 (1952); and to abortion, Planned Parenthood of Southeastern Pa. v. Casey, 505 U.S. 833 (1992).

[12] 539 U.S. 558 (2003).

[13] Id. at 578 stating that:

> The petitioners are entitled to respect for their private lives. The State cannot demean or control their destiny by making their private sexual conduct a crime. The right to liberty under the Due Process Clause gives them the full right to engage in their conduct without the intervention of the government. It is a promise of the Constitution that there is a realm

of personal liberty which the government cannot enter. The Texas statute furthers no legitimate state interest which can justify its intrusion into the personal and private life of the individual.

[14] See e.g., Zablocki v. Redhail, 434 U.S. 347 (1978) (invalidating a Wisconsin statute that required any Wisconsin resident to prove compliance with any support obligation for non-custodial children); Turner v. Safley, 482 U.S. 78 (1987)(invalidating a Missouri regulation that prohibited inmates from marrying unless the prison superintendent approved of the marriage).

[15] 388 U.S. 1 (1967).

[16] Id. at 12.

[17] 133 S.Ct. at 2696. Section 2 was not challenged.

[18] P.L. 104-199, 110 Stat. 2419 (codified at 1 U.S.C. §7 and 28 U.S.C. §1738C).

[19] 28 U.S.C. §1738C states:

No State, territory, or possession of the United States, or Indian tribe, shall be required to give effect to any public act, record, or judicial proceeding of any other State, territory, possession, or tribe respecting a relationship between persons of the same sex that is treated as a marriage under the laws of such other State, territory, possession, or tribe, or a right or claim arising from such relationship.

[20] Section 2 was not challenged in Windsor.

[21] 1 U.S.C. §7 stated:

In determining the meaning of any Act of Congress, or of any ruling, regulation, or interpretation of the various administrative bureaus and agencies of the United States, the word "marriage" means only a legal union between one man and one woman as husband and wife, and the word "spouse" refers only to a person of the opposite sex who is a husband or a wife.

[22] Windsor v. United States, No. 10 Civ. 8435 (S.D.N.Y. June 6, 2012).

[23] 133 S.Ct. at 2694.

[24] Id. at 2693.

[25] Id. at 2696.

[26] Id. at 2696 (Chief Justice Roberts, dissenting)(stating that [t]he Court does not have before it, and the logic of its opinion does not decide, the distinct question whether the States, in the exercise of their "historic and essential authority to define the marital relation," ante, at 2692," may continue to utilize the traditional definition of marriage.").

[27] Id. at 2710 (Scalia, J., dissenting)(explaining that "the majority arms well every challenger to a state law restricting marriage to its traditional definition" and transposing certain portions of the majority opinion to reveal how it could assist these challengers).

[28] Id. at 2714 (Alito, J., dissenting)(stating that "[w]hat Windsor and the United States seek, therefore, is not the protection of a deeply rooted right but the recognition of a very new right, and they seek this innovation not from a legislative body elected by the people, but from unelected judges.").

[29] Kitchen v. Herbert, No. 13-4178, 2014 WL 2868044, *1, *16 (C.A. 10 (Utah)) (stating "we agree with the multiple district courts that have held that the fundamental right to marry necessarily includes the right to remain married.").

[30] Bostic v. Schaefer, Nos. 14-1167, 14-1169, 14-1173, 2014 WL 3702493 (C.A.4 (Va.)), *1, *13.

[31] Baskin v. Brogan, Nos. 14-2386, 14-2387, 14-2388, 14-2526, 2014 WL 4359059 (C.A.7 (Ind.)), *1 (covering challenges to Indiana and Wisconsin bans).

[32] Kitchen v. Herbert, No. 13-4178, 2014 WL 2868044, *1, *16 (C.A. 10 (Utah)); Bishop v. Smith, Nos. 14-5003, 14- 5006, 2014 WL 3537847 (C.A. 10 (Okla.)).

[33] Kitchen v. Herbert, No. 2:13-cv-217, 2013 WL 6697874, at *1 (D. Utah, December 23, 2013); Bishop v. Holder, No. 04-CV-848-TCK-TLW, 2014 WL 116013, at *1 (N.D. Okla., January 14, 2014); Bostic v. Rainey, Civil No. 2:13cv 395, 2014 WL 561978, at *1 (E.D. Va., February 13, 2014); Deboer v. Snyder, No. 12-CV-10285, 2014 WL 1100794, at *1 (E.D. Mich., March 21, 2014); Latta v. Otter, 2014 WL 1909999, at *1 (D. Idaho 2014); Geiger v. Kitzhaber, 2014 WL 2054264, at *1 (D. Or. May 19, 2014); Wolf v. Walker, 2014 WL 2558444 (W.D. Wis., June 6, 2014); De Leon v. Perry, 975 F.Supp.2d 632 (W.D. Tex., 2014).

[34] No. 13-4178, 2014 WL 2868044, *1, *1 (C.A. 10 (Utah)).

[35] Nos. 14-5003, 14-5006, 2014 WL 3537847 (C.A. 10 (Okla.)).

[36] Nos. 14-1167, 14-1169, 14-1173, 2014 WL 3702493 (C.A.4 (Va.)).

[37] Kitchen v. Herbert, No. 13-4178, 2014 WL 2868044, *1, *1 (C.A. 10 (Utah)); see also, Bostic v. Schaefer, Nos. 14- 1167, 14-1169, 14-1173, 2014 WL 3702493 (C.A.4 (Va.)), *1, *1; Bishop v. Smith, Nos. 14-5003, 14-5006, 2014 WL 3537847 (C.A. 10 (Okla.)).

[38] Robicheaux v. Caldwell, Nos. 13-5090, 14-97, 14-327, 2014 WL 4347099, *1, *1 (E.D. La. September 3, 2014).

[39] CF, Borman v. Plyes-Borman, No.2014CV36 located at http://sblog.s3.amazonaws.com/wp-content/uploads/2014/ 08/complete-copy-Tennessee-ruling.pdf (last visited August 14, 2014). Tennessee state court finding that the state's Anti-Recognition Law does not violate equal protection using a rational basis analysis.

[40] Loving v. Virginia, 388 U.S. 1 (1967).

[41] Zablocki v. Redhail, 434 U.S. 347 (1978)(invalidating a Wisconsin statute requiring any Wisconsin resident to prove compliance with any support obligation for non-custodial children).

[42] Turner v. Safley, 482 U.S. 78 (1987)(invalidating a Missouri regulation prohibiting inmates from marrying without the prison superintendent's approval).

[43] Bostic v. Schaefer, Nos. 14-1167, 14-1169, 14-1173, 2014 WL 3702493 (C.A.4 (Va.)), *1, *13.

[44] CF, Robicheaux v. Caldwell, Nos. 13-5090, 14-97, 14-327, 2014 WL 4347099, *1, fn 13 (E.D. La. September 3, 2014)(distinguishing listed cases).

[45] Id. at *6 - *8 (E.D. La. September 3, 2014)(upholding Louisiana's prohibition and non-recognition of same-sex marriage using a rational basis analysis as the relevant provisions do not implicate the fundamental right to marry).

[46] Id. at *8 (stating that "Louisiana has a legitimate interest...whether obsolete in the opinion of some, or not, in the opinion of other ... in linking children to an intact family formed by their two biological parents, as specifically underscored by Justice Kennedy in Windsor.").

[47] Kitchen v. Herbert, 2014 WL 2868044, at *30.

[48] Nos. 14-2386, 14-2387, 14-2388, 14-2526, 2014 WL 4359059 (C.A.7 (Ind.)), *1 (covering challenges to Indiana and Wisconsin bans).

[49] Id at*1, *5.

[50] Id. (stating that "[t]he challenged laws discriminate against a minority defined by an immutable characteristic, and the only rationale that the states put forth with any conviction—that same-sex couples and their children don't need marriage because same-sex couples can't produce children, intended or unintended—is so full of holes that it cannot be taken seriously."); see also, Latta v. Otter, No. 14-35420, 2014 WL 4977682, *1, *1 (C.A. 9 (Idaho)) (finding that states' (Idaho and Nevada) bans on same-sex marriage fail to further

any legitimate purpose, unjustifiably discriminate on the basis of sexual orientation, and are in violation of the Equal Protection Clause).

[51] Id.

[52] CRS Report R43157, The Potential Federal Tax Implications of United States v. Windsor (Striking Section 3 of the Defense of Marriage Act (DOMA)): Selected Issues, by Margot L. Crandall-Hollick, Molly F. Sherlock, and Carol A. Pettit.

In: The Legalization of Same-Sex Marriage
Editor: Kendra Vasquez
ISBN: 978-1-63483-942-6

Chapter 2

SAME-SEX MARRIAGE: A LEGAL OVERVIEW*

Rodney M. Perry

SUMMARY

Same-sex marriage has engendered heated debate throughout the country. There is no federal same-sex marriage prohibition after the Supreme Court's decision in *United States v. Windsor*, which struck down the portion of the Defense of Marriage Act that defined marriage as a union between a man and a woman. However, many states have passed statutes or constitutional amendments that prohibit same-sex couples from marrying, and that deny recognition of same-sex marriages that were legally formed in other states. These state same-sex marriage bans may impact gay individuals' rights and claims to state and federal benefits. For example, such restrictions may affect tax liabilities and entitlements to Social Security.

Until recently, state same-sex marriage bans were seemingly insulated from Fourteenth Amendment challenges in federal courts because of a 1972 Supreme Court decision, *Baker v. Nelson*, wherein the Court summarily dismissed such a challenge for lack of a substantial federal question. However, in recent years, some courts have held that Supreme Court decisions subsequent to *Baker*—namely, *Romer v. Evans*,

* This is an edited, reformatted and augmented version of a Congressional Research Service publication R43886, prepared for Members and Committees of Congress, dated April 6, 2015.

Lawrence v. Texas, and *Windsor*—have rendered *Baker* non-binding. These courts have thus considered whether state same-sex marriage bans violate the Fourteenth Amendment.

Under the Fourteenth Amendment's Equal Protection Clause, state action that classifies groups of individuals may be subject to heightened levels of judicial scrutiny, depending on the type of classification involved. State same-sex marriage bans have faced equal protection challenges because they classify individuals based on sexual orientation. Additionally, under the Fourteenth Amendment's substantive due process guarantees, state action that infringes upon a fundamental right—such as the right to marry—is subject to a high level of judicial scrutiny. State same-sex marriage bans have been challenged on the basis that they infringe upon the fundamental right to marry, which, it has been argued, incorporates the right to same-sex marriage.

Circuit courts are currently split regarding whether *Baker* precludes them from considering the constitutionality of state same-sex marriage bans, and whether such bans violate the Fourteenth Amendment. The Fourth, Seventh, Ninth, and Tenth Circuits have struck down state same-sex marriage bans after finding that Supreme Court decisions subsequent to *Baker* render that decision non-binding. In doing so, they have generally, though not uniformly, subjected state same-sex marriage bans to heightened levels of judicial scrutiny after finding that governmental classifications based on sexual orientation warrant increased scrutiny or finding that the fundamental right to marry includes the right to same-sex marriage.

The Sixth Circuit, on the other hand, held that *Baker* remains binding precedent that precluded its review of Fourteenth Amendment challenges to state same-sex marriage bans. The Sixth Circuit then went on to find that even if it could consider the constitutionality of such bans, it would subject them to the lowest level of judicial scrutiny and uphold them as constitutional. On January 16, 2015, the Supreme Court granted review of cases from the Sixth Circuit involving Fourteenth Amendment challenges to state same-sex marriage bans, with oral arguments scheduled for April 28, 2015. The Court seems poised not only to resolve the existing circuit split, but also to settle key questions about rights for gay people.

Same-sex marriage has engendered heated debate throughout the country. Many states have passed statutes or constitutional amendments that prohibit same-sex couples from marrying, and that deny recognition of same-sex marriages that were legally formed in other states.[1] These same-sex marriage bans may impact gay individuals' rights and claims to state and federal benefits. For example, they may affect tax liabilities and entitlements to Social Security benefits.

Until recently, state same-sex marriage bans were seemingly insulated from Fourteenth Amendment equal protection and due process challenges to their validity because of a 1972 Supreme Court case, *Baker v. Nelson*.[2] There, the Supreme Court dismissed equal protection and due process challenges to a state statute that defined marriage in terms of a man and a woman, finding that the issues involved in the case did not present a substantial federal question.[3]

After *Baker*, state same-sex marriage bans went largely uncontested in federal courts until the Supreme Court relied, in part, on equal protection and due process principles to invalidate a portion of the federal Defense of Marriage Act (DOMA) in *United States v. Windsor*.[4] *Windsor* cast doubt upon whether the Supreme Court finds that equal protection and due process challenges to state same-sex marriage bans still pose no substantial federal questions in accordance with *Baker*. Additionally, though a federal statute was at issue in *Windsor*, that case raised questions regarding the validity of state same-sex marriage bans under the Constitution's equal protection and due process guarantees. Lower courts were left to grapple with these questions, resulting in a circuit split that the Supreme Court appears poised to resolve this term.

This report provides background on, and analysis of, significant legal issues surrounding the same-sex marriage debate. It begins by providing background on the constitutional principles that are often invoked in attempting to invalidate same-sex marriage bans—namely, equal protection and due process guarantees. Then, it discusses key cases that led to the existing circuit split on the constitutionality of state same-sex marriage bans. Finally, this report explains the central issues in the circuit split and analyzes how the Supreme Court might resolve them on appeal.

GENERAL CONSTITUTIONAL PRINCIPLES

Equal Protection

Under the Fourteenth Amendment's Equal Protection Clause, "[n]o State shall ... deny to any person within its jurisdiction the equal protection of the laws."[5] Though there is no parallel constitutional provision expressly prohibiting the federal government from denying equal protection of the law, the Supreme Court has held that equal protection principles similarly apply to the federal government.[6] Under the Constitution's equal protection guarantees, when courts review governmental action that distinguishes between classes of people, they apply different levels of scrutiny depending on the classification involved. The more suspect the government's classification, or the more likely that the government's classification was motivated by discrimination, the higher the level of scrutiny that courts will utilize in evaluating the government's action.[7] Generally speaking, there are three such levels of scrutiny: (1) strict scrutiny; (2) intermediate scrutiny; and (3) rational basis review.

Strict scrutiny is the most searching form of judicial review. The Supreme Court has observed that strict scrutiny applies to governmental classifications that are constitutionally "suspect," or that interfere with fundamental rights.[8] In determining whether a classification is suspect, courts consider whether the classified group: (1) has historically been subject to discrimination; (2) is a minority group exhibiting an unchangeable characteristic that establishes the group as distinct; or (3) is inadequately protected by the political process.[9] There are generally three governmental classifications that are suspect—those based on race, national origin, and alienage.[10] When applying strict scrutiny to governmental action, reviewing courts consider whether the governmental action is *narrowly tailored* to a *compelling* governmental interest.[11] The government bears the burden of proving the constitutional validity of its action under strict scrutiny and, in doing so, must generally show that it cannot meet its goals via less discriminatory means.[12]

Intermediate scrutiny is less searching than strict scrutiny, though it subjects governmental action to more stringent inspection than rational basis review. Intermediate scrutiny applies to "quasi-suspect" classifications, such as classifications based on gender[13] or illegitimacy.[14] When reviewing courts apply intermediate scrutiny to governmental action, they determine whether the action is *substantially related* to achieving an *important* government interest.[15] As with strict scrutiny, the government bears the burden of establishing the constitutional validity of its actions under intermediate scrutiny.[16]

Rational basis review is the least searching form of judicial scrutiny and generally applies to all classifications that are not subject to heightened levels of scrutiny.[17] For governmental action to survive rational basis review, it must be *rationally* related to a *legitimate* government interest.[18] When evaluating governmental action under rational basis review, courts consider the legitimacy of any possible governmental purpose behind the action.[19] That is, courts are not limited to considering the actual purposes behind the government's action.[20] Additionally, the governmental action needs only be a reasonable way of achieving a legitimate government purpose to survive rational basis review; it does not need to be the most reasonable way of doing so, or even more reasonable than alternatives.[21] Accordingly, rational basis review is deferential to the government, and courts generally presume that governmental action that is subject to such review is constitutionally valid.[22] Parties challenging governmental actions bear the burden of establishing their invalidity under rational basis review.[23]

Parties seeking to invalidate same-sex marriage bans have often argued that such bans violate the Constitution's equal protection principles by suggesting that governmental classifications based on sexual orientation are suspect or quasi-suspect, and thus are subject to heightened scrutiny. Conversely, others have argued that such bans are only subject to rational basis review. As discussed below, there is a circuit split as to whether state same-sex marriage bans violate the Constitution's equal protection principles. A similar disagreement exists over whether or not such bans violate the Constitution's substantive due process principles.

Substantive due Process

The U.S. Constitution's due process guarantees are contained within two separate clauses; one can be found in the Fifth Amendment, and the other resides in the Fourteenth Amendment. Each clause provides that the government shall not deprive a person of "life, liberty, or property, without due process of law."[24] However, the Fifth Amendment applies to action by the federal government, whereas the Fourteenth Amendment applies to state action.[25]

The Constitution's due process language makes clear that the government cannot deprive individuals of life, liberty, or property without observing certain procedural requirements. The Supreme Court has interpreted this language to also include substantive guarantees that prohibit the government from taking action that unduly burdens certain liberty interests.[26] More specifically, substantive due process protects against undue governmental infringement upon fundamental rights.[27] To this end, the Supreme Court has held that governmental action infringing upon fundamental rights is subject to strict scrutiny,[28] and thus must be *narrowly tailored* to a *compelling* governmental interest.[29]

Under strict scrutiny, the government must generally show that it has a "substantial" and "legitimate" need for its action to be in furtherance of a compelling government interest.[30] If the government successfully establishes a compelling interest, its action cannot encumber fundamental rights any more than is necessary to achieve the government's need.[31] Additionally, the government could not have possibly taken alternative action that would similarly further its interest while being less burdensome on fundamental rights.[32] Otherwise, the government's action is not narrowly tailored to the government's interest.[33]

The Supreme Court has recognized a number of rights as fundamental, including the right to have children,[34] use contraception,[35] and marry.[36] Generally, when parties have sought the invalidation of same-sex marriage bans under the Constitution's substantive due process guarantees, they have argued that prohibiting same-sex couples from marrying infringes upon the fundamental right to marry. The circuit courts have split regarding whether state same-sex marriage bans violate the Fourteenth Amendment's guarantees, and in doing so, they have interpreted Supreme Court precedent in differing ways.

THE SUPREME COURT PRECEDENT CONTRIBUTING TO THE CIRCUIT SPLIT

Until recently, state same-sex marriage bans were seemingly insulated from Fourteenth Amendment equal protection and due process challenges by the Supreme Court's decision in *Baker v. Nelson*.[37] In *Baker*, a same-sex couple challenged a Minnesota statute before the Minnesota Supreme Court, arguing that the statute, which referred to marriage as between a "husband and wife," violated the Constitution's due process and equal protection principles.[38] More specifically, the plaintiffs argued that substantive due process's protection of the fundamental right to marry applied equally to opposite-sex and same-sex couples, and that prohibiting same-sex marriages denies those in same-sex relationships equal protection of the law.[39] The Minnesota Supreme Court rejected both of these arguments. According to the court, the fundamental right to marry did not include the right of same-sex couples to marry,[40] and Minnesota's classification of persons who are authorized to marry did not offend the Constitution's equal protection principles.[41] The court seemingly utilized rational basis review, and rested its conclusion on the fact that Minnesota did not classify those authorized to marry with any "irrational or invidious discrimination."[42]

The plaintiffs in *Baker* then appealed to the U.S. Supreme Court, which was required to grant review under a now-defunct statute mandating that the Court accept appeals of state supreme court cases wherein state statutes face constitutional challenges.[43] The plaintiffs' appeal asked the Supreme Court to consider whether Minnesota's refusal to recognize their marriage: (1) deprived them of due process of the law under the Fourteenth Amendment; (2) violated their rights under the Fourteenth Amendment's Equal Protection Clause; or (3) deprived them of their right to privacy under the Ninth and Fourteenth Amendments.[44] The Supreme Court summarily dismissed the appeal, that is, dismissed it without an opinion "for want of [a] substantial federal question."[45]

A summary dismissal is considered a decision on a case's merits, and is thus binding on lower courts.[46] That is, a summary dismissal rejects the specific issues challenging an appealed decision, and this dismissal creates precedent that lower federal courts must then follow when considering the same issues.[47] Therefore, in the immediate wake of the Supreme Court's summary dismissal in *Baker*, it appeared as though lower federal courts had to dismiss challenges to state same-sex marriage bans that were based on the Constitution's equal protection and due process principles. However, the Supreme Court has also held that summary dismissals are no longer binding precedent when doctrinal developments show that the Court now views the issues summarily decided as raising "substantial federal question[s]."[48]

The circuit courts that have considered equal protection and due process challenges to state same-sex marriage bans are split regarding whether *Baker* requires them to dismiss such claims. The U.S. Court of Appeals for the Sixth Circuit (Sixth Circuit) has held that *Baker* precludes it from evaluating equal protection and due process challenges to state same-sex marriages.[49] Conversely, the U.S. Courts of Appeals for the Fourth,[50] Seventh,[51] Ninth,[52] and Tenth[53] Circuits have all held that doctrinal developments since *Baker*—more specifically, the Supreme Court's decisions in *Romer v. Evans*,[54] *Lawrence v. Texas*,[55] and *United States v. Windsor*[56]—indicate that the Court now views the issues summarily decided in *Baker* as raising substantial federal questions. Accordingly, these circuit courts have held that *Baker* does not preclude their review of equal protection and due process challenges to state same-sex marriage bans.

Romer v. Evans

In *Romer v. Evans* (1996), the Supreme Court was tasked with determining whether a Colorado constitutional amendment, which prohibited all legislative, executive, or judicial action designed to protect gay people from discrimination, violated the Fourteenth Amendment's Equal Protection Clause. The Court observed that governmental action that does not burden a fundamental right or target a suspect class receives rational basis review, and thus must be upheld so long as the government's classification is rationally related to a legitimate government interest.[57] Though the Court did not state that gay individuals are not a suspect class or that the Colorado amendment at issue did not burden a fundamental right, it may have implicitly declared as much by seemingly using a form of rational basis review when evaluating the amendment.[58] According to the Court, the requirement that governmental classifications be rationally related to a legitimate governmental interest ensures that governmental classifications are not intended to disadvantage a particular group.[59]

Colorado argued that its constitutional amendment did nothing more than deny special protections to individuals who are gay, and thereby put them in the same position as all other people.[60] The Court disagreed, observing that the amendment imposed a "broad and undifferentiated" disability on gay people, the breadth of which was incongruent with the state's proffered rationale of denying special rights to such individuals.[61] According to the Court, the Colorado constitutional amendment could only have been enacted out of animus toward individuals who are gay, and thus was not rationally related to a legitimate state interest.[62] As such, the Court invalidated the amendment.[63]

Lawrence v. Texas

The Supreme Court seemingly expanded the rights of gay people under substantive due process principles in *Lawrence v. Texas* (2003). At issue in *Lawrence* was a Texas statute that criminalized same-sex sexual contact.[64] The plaintiffs were two gay men who were arrested and convicted of violating the statute.[65] The Court considered whether the Texas statute violated the Fourteenth Amendment's substantive due process protections. Previously, in *Bowers v. Hardwick*[66] (1986), the Supreme Court had held that a similar state statute did not violate substantive due process principles after finding that the fundamental right to privacy does not extend to homosexual sodomy.[67] Because it found no fundamental right at issue, the Court in *Bowers* then applied rational basis review in upholding the statute.[68] In doing so, the Court seemingly found that states can have a legitimate interest in upholding majority notions of morality, and that the sodomy statute at issue was rationally related to this interest.[69]

Justice Kennedy's majority opinion in *Lawrence* explicitly overruled *Bowers*.[70] In so doing, the Court stated that liberty protections arising from substantive due process extend to private sexual relationships between two consenting adults, including individuals who are gay.[71] As such, the Court held that gay people have the "full right" to engage in private, consensual sexual conduct.[72] However, the Court did not clarify the proper level of scrutiny to be used when considering laws that prohibit consensual sexual activity between such individuals. At no point in the opinion did the Court determine whether the right of gay people to engage in sexual activity is a fundamental right, nor did it mention strict scrutiny or rational basis review. The closest the Court came to doing so appears toward the end of the majority opinion, when the Court stated, "The Texas statute furthers no legitimate state interest which can justify its intrusion into the personal and private life of the individuals."[73]

This language suggests that the Court may have applied a version of rational basis review, which requires a showing that the statute is rationally related to a legitimate government interest. Even so, *Lawrence* marks an advancement in the rights of gay individuals as it was the first time that the Court recognized that the Constitution's substantive due process protections can extend to same-sex sexual activity.

United States v. Windsor

In *United States v. Windsor* (2013), the Supreme Court struck down Section 3 of the federal Defense of Marriage Act (DOMA), which required marriage to be defined as the union of one man and one woman for purposes of federal laws and regulations.[74] In doing so, the Court relied on equal protection and due process considerations, along with the federalism-based rationale that marriage is an area historically left to state regulation.

The plaintiff in *Windsor* and her late spouse were New York residents whose same-sex marriage was legally recognized in New York, though they were married elsewhere.[75] The deceased spouse left her entire estate to the plaintiff.[76] However, because of DOMA, the deceased spouse's estate could not claim the marital exemption from the federal estate tax and paid $363,053 in taxes, leading the plaintiff to seek a tax refund.[77] The Internal Revenue Service denied the refund, determining that the plaintiff was not a "surviving spouse" under DOMA.[78] The plaintiff subsequently filed suit, claiming that DOMA violated the Fifth Amendment's Equal Protection Clause.[79]

In finding Section 3 of DOMA unconstitutional, Justice Kennedy's majority opinion raised principles of federalism by examining the historical relationship between the federal and state governments concerning domestic relations. The Court observed that marriage was traditionally regulated by the states, and that states had "historic and essential" authority to define marital relations, subject to the limits of constitutional guarantees.[80] The Court then seemingly took issue with the fact that DOMA departs from this historical practice of relying on state definitions of marriage.[81]

The Court also considered equal protection and due process principles in invalidating Section 3. The Court observed that the Fifth Amendment prohibits congressional action that subjects a politically unpopular group to disparate treatment for the purpose of harming that group.[82] The purpose of DOMA, the Court found, was to disadvantage and stigmatize same-sex marriages, as evidenced by the statute's legislative history, text, and primary effect.[83] By attempting to injure same-sex married couples, which New York sought to protect, the Court determined that DOMA "violate[d] basic due process and equal protection principles applicable to the Federal Government."[84]

While the Court resolved the question of the constitutionality of a federal definition of marriage that excludes same-sex couples in *Windsor*, it left a number of unanswered questions. Though it is clear that federalism played a role in the Court's decision, it is unclear just how determinative it was toward the outcome. For example, Justice Roberts, dissenting in *Windsor*, seemingly suggests that federalism played a key role in the majority's opinion, observing that the state's traditional power to define marital relations was of "central relevance" to the majority's decision to invalidate DOMA.[85] Conversely, Justice Scalia, dissenting in *Windsor*, seemingly suggests that federalism played a smaller role in the majority's opinion, noting that the majority opinion "formally disclaim[s] reliance upon principles of federalism" at one point.[86] This apparent ambiguity has contributed to differing outcomes when lower courts have considered state same-sex marriage bans, as discussed in more depth below, because such state bans lack the federalism implications of a federal statute like DOMA. Additionally, the Court did not address whether same-sex couples have a fundamental right to marry, or whether sexual orientation classifications warrant heightened scrutiny. In *Windsor*'s wake, lower courts were left to grapple with these issues.

Current Circuit Split

In the wake of *Windsor*, a number of challenges to state same-sex marriage bans made their way into federal courts. These courts have generally been tasked with determining whether, as an initial matter, *Baker* precludes their review of state same-sex marriage bans, or whether doctrinal developments after that case—namely, *Romer*, *Lawrence*, and *Windsor*—render it non-binding. These courts have also considered the appropriate level of scrutiny for classifications based on sexual orientation required under the Constitution's equal protection principles, and whether the fundamental right to marry under the Constitution's due process principles incorporates same-sex marriage. In resolving these questions, a circuit split developed.

Four Circuits Strike Down State Same-Sex Marriage Bans

The U.S. Courts of Appeals for the Fourth, Seventh, Ninth, and Tenth Circuits have all invalidated state same-sex marriage bans. In doing so, they have each determined that doctrinal developments subsequent to *Baker* render that decision non-binding.[87] More specifically, they have held that doctrinal developments after *Baker*—primarily the Supreme Court's decisions in *Romer*, *Lawrence*, and *Windsor*—make clear that the issue of whether state same-sex marriage bans violate the Fourteenth Amendment's equal protection and due process principles does, in fact, raise a substantial federal question.[88]

For example, the U.S. Court of Appeals for the Fourth Circuit (Fourth Circuit) in *Bostic v. Schaefer* found the Supreme Court's development of its equal protection and due process jurisprudence after *Baker* demonstrates that *Baker* is no longer binding precedent.[89] Regarding due process, the Fourth Circuit observed that *Lawrence* and *Windsor* "firmly position same-sex relationships within the ambit of the Due Process Clauses' protection," contrary to *Baker*.[90] The Fourth Circuit similarly found that Supreme Court equal protection cases, including *Romer* and *Windsor*, show that the court has substantially changed the way it considers sex and sexual orientation in the equal protection context.[91]

After concluding that they are not bound by *Baker*, the Fourth, Seventh, Ninth, and Tenth Circuits then turned to the question of whether state same-sex marriage bans violate the Fourteenth Amendment's equal protection or due process principles. On the one hand, the Fourth, Ninth, and Tenth Circuits have all subjected state same-sex marriage bans to heightened levels of scrutiny after finding that such bans infringe upon fundamental rights or create suspect classifications. The Seventh Circuit, on the other hand, used rational basis review when invalidating state same-sex marriage bans.

In *Bostic*, the Fourth Circuit held that the fundamental right to marry includes the right of same-sex couples to marry.[92] According to the Fourth Circuit, the right to marry belongs to each individual and is not restricted by the characteristics of the individual seeking to utilize it.[93] This result, the Fourth Circuit suggested, is supported by Supreme Court precedent. For example, the Fourth Circuit observed that in *Lawrence*, the Supreme Court did not determine that the right at issue was the right of gay people to engage in sodomy, but rather the right of all people, including individuals who are gay, to make decisions regarding their sexual relationships.[94] After determining that the fundamental right to marriage includes same-sex marriage and observing that state same-sex marriage bans significantly infringe upon this right, the Fourth Circuit applied strict scrutiny and invalidated such bans.[95]

In invalidating state same-sex marriage bans, the U.S. Court of Appeals for the Tenth Circuit (Tenth Circuit) similarly relied on the fundamental right to marry in *Kitchen v. Herbert* and *Bishop v. Smith*. In *Kitchen*, the Tenth Circuit held that the fundamental right to marry is properly considered broadly as the right of the individual to marry, rather than narrowly as the right of opposite-sex couples to marry.[96] The Tenth Circuit followed *Kitchen*'s holding in *Bishop*.[97] As such, it applied strict scrutiny in both cases.[98] In both cases, the Tenth Circuit held that state same-sex marriage bans were not narrowly tailored to compelling government interests, and thus invalidated such bans.[99]

In *Latta v. Otter*, the U.S. Court of Appeals for the Ninth Circuit (Ninth Circuit), like the Fourth and Tenth Circuits, subjected state same-sex marriage bans to heightened scrutiny. However, the Ninth Circuit's majority opinion in *Latta* differed from the Fourth and Tenth Circuit opinions as it relied on equal protection principles. The Ninth Circuit observed that equal protection guarantees require classifications based on sexual orientation to be subject to heightened scrutiny, but did not consider whether the fundamental right to marriage includes the right to same-sex marriage.[100]

The U.S. Court of Appeals for the Seventh Circuit (Seventh Circuit)—unlike the Fourth, Ninth, and Tenth Circuits—did not apply heightened scrutiny in striking down state same-sex marriage bans in *Baskin v. Bogan*. The Seventh Circuit held that state same-sex marriage bans cannot survive rational basis review as "[t]he discrimination against same-sex couples is irrational, and therefore unconstitutional even if the discrimination is not subjected to heightened scrutiny...."[101] The Seventh Circuit observed that because such bans cannot pass constitutional muster under equal protection principles, it had no reason to reach the question of whether or not the fundamental right to marriage includes the right to same-sex marriage for purposes of the due process clause.[102]

The Sixth Circuit Upholds State Same-Sex Marriage Bans

Unlike the Fourth, Seventh, Ninth, and Tenth Circuits, when tasked with evaluating the constitutionality of four state same-sex marriage bans, the U.S. Court of Appeals for the Sixth Circuit (Sixth Circuit) upheld such bans in *DeBoer v. Snyder*.[103] As an initial matter, the Sixth Circuit considered whether *Baker* prevented it from determining whether state same-sex marriage bans violate the Fourteenth Amendment. The plaintiffs argued that *Windsor* limited *Baker*'s applicability, and thus that the Sixth Circuit was not bound by *Baker*.[104] The Sixth Circuit disagreed.[105] According to the Sixth Circuit, the outcomes and rationales of *Baker* and *Windsor* are not inconsistent.[106] More specifically, the Sixth Circuit reasoned that in invalidating Section 3 of DOMA, *Windsor* turned on the fact that DOMA, as a federal law, infringed on state authority over marital relations, while *Baker* upheld the right of a state's people to define marriage.[107]

The plaintiffs then argued that, if *Windsor* did not overrule *Baker*, doctrinal developments since *Baker* (including *Romer*, *Lawrence*, and *Windsor*) render that case non-binding.[108] According to the Sixth Circuit, it can only disregard summary dismissals in two circumstances: (1) when a Supreme Court decision overrules the summary dismissal by name; and (2) when the Supreme Court overrules the summary dismissal by outcome.[109] The Sixth Circuit held that neither circumstance had occurred, finding that nothing in *Romer*, *Lawrence*, or *Windsor* expressly overruled *Baker*, nor was any of the three inconsistent with *Baker*'s outcome.[110] Though the Sixth Circuit observed that it was bound by *Baker*, it did discuss whether state same-sex marriage bans violate the Fourteenth Amendment's equal protection and due process guarantees.

The Sixth Circuit determined that state same-sex marriage bans are subject to rational basis review when analyzed under either equal protection or substantive due process guarantees of the Fourteenth Amendment. Regarding equal protection, the Sixth Circuit observed that the Supreme Court has never held that classifications based on sexual orientation are suspect or entitled to heightened review.[111] The Sixth Circuit also noted that its precedents have held that classifications based on sexual orientation receive rational basis review.[112] Regarding substantive due process, the Sixth Circuit determined that the fundamental right to marry does not include the right to same-sex marriage.[113]

In applying rational basis review to state same-sex marriage bans, the Sixth Circuit observed that the standard is highly deferential to the government.[114] However, the Sixth Circuit did observe that governmental action motivated by animus toward a particular group of people cannot pass rational basis review.[115] The state same-sex marriage bans at issue in the case, the Sixth Circuit observed, were constitutional amendments voted on by the citizens of each respective state.[116] The Sixth Circuit reasoned that it could not attribute one motivation—animus—to all of the voters in each state that wished to pass same-sex marriage bans, and thus found no animus present.[117] The Sixth Circuit determined that state same-sex marriage bans are rationally related to two legitimate state interests: (1) incentivizing people who procreate to stay together during child rearing; and (2) the desire to "wait and see" before changing marriage norms that have existed for centuries.[118] Accordingly, the Sixth Circuit found that such bans survive rational basis review.[119]

Supreme Court Appears Poised to Resolve the Circuit Split

On January 16, 2015, the Supreme Court announced that it was consolidating and granting review of the four state same-sex marriage ban cases that the Sixth Circuit decided in *DeBoer v. Snyder*.[120] Oral arguments are scheduled for April 28, 2015. On appeal, the Court will be considering two questions:

1. Does the Fourteenth Amendment require a state to license a marriage between two people of the same sex?
2. Does the Fourteenth Amendment require a state to recognize a marriage between two people of the same sex when their marriage was lawfully licensed and performed out-of-state?

Commentators have remarked on the likelihood that a final ruling on these two questions will result in a split vote, with Justice Kennedy's vote determinative.[121] In answering these two questions, the Court could reach one of multiple conclusions. These possibilities are outlined below.

The Court Could Arguably Uphold State Same-Sex Marriage Bans

The Court could, for example, potentially decide that the Fourteenth Amendment does not require states to permit same-sex marriages nor to recognize same-sex marriages that were lawfully licensed and performed out-of-state. If the Court were to reach this conclusion, it could arguably do so by finding that state same-sex marriage bans neither create suspect or quasi-suspect classifications, nor infringe upon fundamental rights, and thus are not subject to heightened scrutiny under the Fourteenth Amendment's equal protection and due process guarantees, just as the Sixth Circuit did in *DeBoer*. In line with *DeBoer*, the Court might find that because the state same-sex marriage bans at issue were enacted through majority vote of state citizens, who presumably had varying motivations, the bans were not driven by animus toward gay individuals. The Court might then, as in *DeBoer*, find that state statutes and constitutional amendments that prohibit same-sex marriages and deny recognition of same-sex marriages legally formed in other states are rationally related to legitimate state interests. If the Court were to reach this outcome, states with same-sex marriage bans—including those whose bans had been struck down by lower federal courts—could potentially prohibit same-sex couples from marrying and refuse to recognize same-sex marriages legally formed in other states.

The Court Could Arguably Invalidate State Same-Sex Marriage Bans

In the alternative, the Court could potentially hold that the Fourteenth Amendment requires states to permit same-sex marriages and to recognize same-sex marriages legally performed in other states. The immediate effect of such a ruling would be that same-sex marriages would be legal in all states. However, the Court's rationale in reaching such a result would arguably be significant: the Court could reach its conclusion in a way that has implications for the constitutional guarantees for gay people outside of the marriage context, or it could limit its decision to only expand the rights of such individuals within the marriage context.

For example, the Court might follow the approach of the Ninth Circuit and determine that classifications based on sexual orientation are subject to heightened scrutiny. Such a holding would arguably be broad, and would seem to subject *all* laws classifying individuals based on sexual orientation—not only those pertaining to the ability of same-sex couples to marry—to heightened constitutional scrutiny. Accordingly, such an approach seemingly could increase the constitutional rights of gay people not just with regard to marriage, but in other areas as well.

On the other hand, the Court might conclude that the Fourteenth Amendment requires states to permit same-sex marriages and recognize same-sex marriages legally formed in other states on narrower grounds, which could limit its holding. For example, the Court might hold, as the Fourth and Tenth Circuits have ruled, that the fundamental right to marry includes the right to same-sex marriage. Such a finding would appear only to expand the rights of gay people within the marriage context.

A further alternative might find the Court subjecting state same-sex marriage bans to rational basis review, but concluding that they do not meet the requirements of this test, as the Seventh Circuit has. In invalidating state same-sex marriage bans under rational basis review, the Court might find that such bans are motivated by animus, similar to the state constitutional amendment at issue in *Romer*, and thus potentially find that states lacked a legitimate interest in enacting them. Such an approach could be perceived, particularly when considered with *Romer*, as a signal that the Court may apply a less deferential version of rational basis review when considering governmental action that harms individuals who are gay. However, such a finding could also just be illustrative of the fact that the Court arguably finds state same-sex marriage bans and the law at issue in *Romer* irrational.

The Court Could Resolve Each Question Differently

As a final alternative, the Court could hold that states are not required to permit same-sex marriages to be formed in the states, but must recognize same-sex marriages lawfully formed in other states. Under this analysis, the Court might, for example, invoke principles of federalism, just as it did in *Windsor*, to essentially say that states have autonomy in defining who can get married within their borders, but cannot disregard other states' decisions to allow same-sex marriages.

CONCLUSION

The Supreme Court appears poised to resolve the question of the constitutionality of state same-sex marriage bans. On the one hand, if the Court were to uphold state same-sex marriage bans, then same-sex couples could not get married in states with such bans enacted. Such a decision could also invalidate the marriages of same-sex couples who were married in response to lower courts striking down their states' same-sex marriage bans. On the other hand, if the Court were to find that state same-sex marriage bans are unconstitutional, it would seemingly broaden the rights of gay individuals by permitting same-sex marriages in all states. Such a result could extend certain state and federal benefits that accompany marriage to same-sex couples that currently lack access to them.

End Notes

[1] See, e.g., Mich. Const. art. I, §25 (Michigan constitutional amendment defining marriage as "the union of one man and one woman" and denying recognition of same-sex marriages performed in other states); Ky. Const. §233A (Kentucky constitutional amendment defining marriage as "between one man and one woman" and denying recognition of same-sex marriages performed in other states).

[2] 409 U.S. 810 (1972). See infra notes 37-56 and accompanying text.

[3] Baker, 409 U.S. at 810.

[4] 133 S. Ct. 2675 (2013).

[5] U.S. Const. amend. XIV, §1.

[6] See Bolling v. Sharpe, 347 U.S. 497 (1954). More specifically, the Court has held that the Fifth Amendment's guarantee of "due process of the law," applicable to the federal government, incorporates equal protection guarantees. See id. at 500.

[7] Compare City of Cleburne v. Cleburne Living Center, 473 U.S. 432 (1985) (holding that mental disability is not a "quasi-suspect" classification, and thus is entitled to rational basis review) with Graham v. Richardson, 403 U.S. 365 (1971) (holding that classifications based on alienage are "inherently suspect," and are subject to strict scrutiny).

[8] See Mass. Bd. of Retirement v. Murgia, 427 U.S. 307, 312 (1976); see also Heller v. Doe, 509 U.S. 312, 319 (1993).

[9] See Lyng v. Castillo, 477 U.S. 635, 638 (1986); see also United States v. Carolene Prods. Co., 304 U.S. 144, 152 n. 4 (1938).

[10] Graham, 403 U.S. at 371-72 ("... the Court's decisions have established that classifications based on alienage, like those based on nationality or race, are inherently suspect and subject to close judicial scrutiny.").

[11] Parents Involved in Cmty. Schs. v. Seattle Sch. Dist. No. 1, 551 U.S. 701, 720 (2007).

[12] See Fisher v. University of Tex. at Austin, 133 S. Ct. 2411, 2420 (2014).

[13] United States v. Virginia, 518 U.S. 515, 533 (1996); see Miss. Univ. for Women v. Hogan, 458 U.S. 718, 724 (1982).

[14] Clark v. Jeter, 486 U.S. 456, 461 (1988) ("Between these extremes of rational basis review and strict scrutiny lies a level of intermediate scrutiny, which generally has been applied to discriminatory classifications based on sex or illegitimacy.").

[15] See Craig v. Boren, 429 U.S. 190, 198 (1976); see also Clark, 486 U.S. at 461.

[16] Virginia, 518 U.S. at 533; see Miss. Univ. for Women, 458 U.S. at 724.

[17] See Cleburne Living Center, 473 U.S at 440-42; see also Schweiker v. Wilson, 450 U.S. 221, 230 (1981).

[18] See City of Cleburne, 473 U.S. at 440.

[19] See Nordlinger v. Hahn, 505 U.S. 1, 15 (1992); see also Heller, 509 U.S. at 320.

[20] See Nordlinger, 505 U.S. at 15; see also Heller, 509 U.S. at 320.

[21] See Schweiker, 450 U.S. 221, 235 (1981) (observing that, under rational basis review, "[a]s long as the classificatory scheme chosen by Congress rationally advances a reasonable and identifiable governmental objective, we must disregard the existence of other methods of allocation that we, as individuals, perhaps would have preferred."); see also Heller, 509 U.S. at 320 (observing that under rational basis review, "a classification 'must be upheld against equal protection challenge if there is any reasonably conceivable state of facts that could provide a rational basis for the classification.'") (quoting F.C.C. v. Beach Commc'ns,, Inc., 508 U.S. 307, 312 (1993)).

[22] See Beach Commc'ns, Inc., 508 U.S. at 315; see also Murgia, 427 U.S. at 315.

[23] Heller, 509 U.S. at 320 (noting that, when reviewing a governmental classification under rational basis review, a governmental action is "presumed constitutional" and the burden lies on the party attacking the governmental action to establish the action's unconstitutionality.).

[24] U.S. Const. amend. XIV, §1; U.S. Const. amend. V.

[25] See U.S. Const. amend. XIV, §1; U.S. Const. amend. V.

[26] See Washington v. Glucksberg, 512 U.S. 702, 719-720 (1997).

[27] See id.

[28] See Reno v. Flores, 507 U.S. 292, 301-02 (1993).

[29] Id (observing that a line of Supreme Court cases interprets the Fifth and Fourteenth Amendment's due process principles to "forbid[] the government to infringe certain 'fundamental' liberty interests at all ... unless the infringement is narrowly tailored to serve a compelling state interest.").

[30] San Antonio Indep. School Dist. v. Rodriguez, 411 U.S. 1, 98 (1973).

[31] See Dunn v. Blumstein, 405 U.S. 330, 343 (1972).

[32] Id ("if there are other, reasonable ways to achieve [government interests] with a lesser burden on constitutionally protected activity, a State may not choose the way of greater interference. If it acts at all, it must choose 'less drastic means.'") (quoting Shelton v. Tucker, 364 U.S. 479, 488 (1960)).

[33] See id.

[34] Skinner v. Okla., 316 U.S. 535 (1942).

[35] Griswold v. Connecticut, 381 U.S. 479 (1965).

[36] Loving v. Virginia, 388 U.S. 1 (1967).

[37] 409 U.S. 810 (1972).

[38] Baker v. Nelson, 191 N.W.2d 185 (Minn. 1971).

[39] Id. at 186.

[40] Id. at 187.

[41] Id.

[42] Id.

[43] 28 U.S.C. §1257 (1970).

[44] Jurisdictional Statement of Appellants at 3, Baker v. Nelson, 409 U.S. 810 (1972).

[45] Baker, 409 U.S. at 810.

[46] Hicks v. Miranda, 422 U.S. 332, 344 (1975).

[47] See Mandel v. Bradley, 432 U.S. 173, 176 (1977).

[48] See Hicks, 422 U.S. at 344-45.

[49] DeBoer v. Snyder, 772 F.3d 388 (6th Cir. 2014).

[50] Bostic v. Schaefer, 760 F.3d 352 (4th Cir. 2014).

[51] Baskin v. Bogan, 766 F.3d 648 (7th Cir. 2014).

[52] Latta v. Otter, 771 F.3d 456 (9th Cir. 2014).

[53] Bishop v. Smith, 760 F.3d 1070 (10th Cir. 2014); Kitchen v. Herbert, 755 F.3d 1193 (10th Cir. 2014).
[54] 517 U.S. 620 (1996).
[55] 539 U.S. 558 (2003).
[56] 133 S.Ct. 2675 (2013).
[57] Romer, 517 U.S. at 631.
[58] Id.
[59] Id. at 633.
[60] Id. at 626.
[61] Id. at 632.
[62] Id.
[63] Id.
[64] Lawrence, 539 U.S. at 563.
[65] Id. at 563.
[66] 478 U.S. 186 (1986).
[67] Id. at 190.
[68] Id. at 196.
[69] See id.
[70] Lawrence, 539 U.S. at 525 ("Bowers was not correct when it was decided, and it is not correct today. It ought not to remain binding precedent. Bowers v. Hardwick should be and now is overruled.").
[71] Id. at 578.
[72] Id. at 578.
[73] Id.
[74] P.L. 104-199, §3, 110 Stat. 2419, 2419 (1996).
[75] Windsor, 133 S. Ct. at 2683.
[76] Id.
[77] Id.
[78] Id.
[79] Id.
[80] Id. at 2692.
[81] See id.
[82] Id. at 2393.
[83] See id. at 2393-94.
[84] Id. at 2393.
[85] Id. at 2697 (Roberts, J., dissenting).
[86] Id. at 2705 (Scalia, J., dissenting).
[87] Bostic v. Schaefer, 760 F.3d 352, 375 (4th Cir. 2014) ("In light of the Supreme Court's apparent abandonment of Baker and the significant doctrinal developments that occurred after the Court issued its summary dismissal in that case, we decline to view Baker as binding precedent ..."); Baskin v. Bogan, 766 F.3d 648, 660 (7th Cir. 2014) (observing that Romer, Lawrence, and Windsor "make clear that Baker is no longer authoritative); Latta v. Otter, 771 F.3d 456, 466 (9th Cir. 2014); Bishop v. Smith, 760 F.3d 1070, 1080 (10th Cir. 2014); Kitchen v. Herbert, 755 F.3d 1193, 1208 (10th Cir. 2014) ("Although reasonable judges may disagree on the merits of the same-sex marriage question, we think it is clear that doctrinal developments foreclose the conclusion that the issue is, as Baker determined, wholly insubstantial.").

[88] See, e.g., Bishop, 760 F.3d at 1080 (in holding Baker non-binding while considering the constitutionality of a state same-sex marriage ban, noting that "[a]s any observer of the Supreme Court cannot help but realize, this case and others like it present not only substantial but pressing federal questions.").

[89] Bostic, 760 F.3d at 374.

[90] See id.

[91] See id. at 374-75.

[92] Id. at at 376.

[93] See id. at 376-77.

[94] See id. at 377.

[95] Id. at 378, 384.

[96] See Kitchen, 755 F.3d at 1209.

[97] See Bishop, 760 F.3d at 1080.

[98] Kitchen, 755 F.3d at 1218; Bishop, 760 F.3d at 1079.

[99] Kitchen. 755 F.3d at 1229-30; Bishop, 760 F.3d at 1081-82.

[100] See Latta, 771 F.3d at 468. In concurrence, one judge wrote separately to say that he would also have held that the fundamental right to marry includes the right to same-sex marriage. Id. at 477 (Reinhardt, J., concurring).

[101] Baskin, 766 F.3d at 656.

[102] Id. at 657.

[103] 772 F.3d 388 (6th Cir. 2014).

[104] Id. at 400.

[105] Id.

[106] Id.

[107] See id.

[108] Id. at 401.

[109] Id.

[110] See id. at 401-02.

[111] Id. at 413.

[112] Id.

[113] Id. at 411-12.

[114] Id. at 405 ("So long as judges can conceive of some 'plausible' reason for the law—any plausible reason, even one that did not motivate the legislators who enacted it—the law must stand, no matter how unfair, unjust, or unwise the judges may consider it to citizens.") (emphasis in original).

[115] Id. at 408.

[116] Id. at 409.

[117] Id. at 409-10.

[118] Id. at 405-6.

[119] See id. at 406.

[120] Certiorari Granted, Nos. 14-556, 14-562, 14-571, 14-574, available at http://www.supreme court.gov/orders/ courtorders/011615zr_f2q3.pdf.

[121] See, e.g., Ashby Jones, In Same-Sex Cases, Justice Kennedy Likely to Cast Swing Vote, WALL STREET J., January 16, 2015, http://blogs.wsj.com/law/2015/01/16/in-same-sex-cases-eyes-likely-to-swing-to-justice-kennedy/; Richard Wolf, Supreme Court Agrees to Rule on Gay Marriage, USA TODAY, January 16, 2015, http://www.usatoday.com/story/news/nation/2015/01/16/supreme-court-gay-marriage/21867355/.

In: The Legalization of Same-Sex Marriage ISBN: 978-1-63483-942-6
Editor: Kendra Vasquez

Chapter 3

OBERGEFELL V. HODGES: SAME-SEX MARRIAGE LEGALIZED*

Rodney M. Perry

SUMMARY

On June 26, 2015, the Supreme Court issued its decision in *Obergefell v. Hodges* requiring states to issue marriage licenses to same-sex couples and to recognize same-sex marriages that were legally formed in other states. In doing so, the Court resolved a circuit split regarding the constitutionality of state same-sex marriage bans and legalized same-sex marriage throughout the country. The Court's decision relied on the Fourteenth Amendment's equal protection and due process guarantees.

Under the Fourteenth Amendment's Equal Protection Clause, state action that classifies groups of individuals may be subject to heightened levels of judicial scrutiny, depending on the type of classification involved or whether the classification interferes with a fundamental right. Additionally, under the Fourteenth Amendment's substantive due process guarantees, state action that infringes upon a fundamental right—such as the right to marry—is subject to a high level of judicial scrutiny.

In striking down state same-sex marriage bans as unconstitutional in *Obergefell*, the Court rested its decision upon the fundamental right to

* This is an edited, reformatted and augmented version of a Congressional Research Service publication R44143, prepared for Members and Committees of Congress dated August 7, 2015.

marry. The Court acknowledged that its precedents have described the fundamental right to marry in terms of opposite-sex relationships. Even so, the Court determined that the reasons why the right to marry is considered fundamental apply equally to same-sex marriages. The Court thus held that the fundamental right to marry extends to same-sex couples, and that state same-sex marriage bans unconstitutionally interfere with this right.

Though the Supreme Court's decision in *Obergefell* resolved the question of whether or not state same-sex marriage bans are unconstitutional, it raised a number of other questions. These include questions regarding, among other things, *Obergefell*'s broader impact on the rights of gay individuals; the proper level of judicial scrutiny applicable to classifications based on sexual orientation; what the decision might mean for laws prohibiting plural marriages; the Court's approach to recognizing fundamental rights moving forward; and the proper level of judicial scrutiny applicable to governmental action interfering with fundamental rights. This report explores these questions.

On June 26, 2015, the Supreme Court issued its decision in *Obergefell v. Hodges* legalizing same-sex marriage throughout the country by requiring states to issue marriage licenses to same-sex couples and to recognize same-sex marriages that were legally formed in other states. In doing so, the Court resolved a circuit split[1] regarding the constitutionality of state same-sex marriage bans.

This report provides background on, and analysis of, significant legal issues raised by the Supreme Court's decision in *Obergefell.* It first offers background on the constitutional principles on which the Court relied in *Obergefell* to invalidate state same-sex marriage bans as unconstitutional. Then, it walks through the Court's opinion and rationale. Finally, it discusses potential implications of the Court's decision.

General Constitutional Principles

Equal Protection

Under the Fourteenth Amendment's Equal Protection Clause, "[n]o State shall ... deny to any person within its jurisdiction the equal protection of the laws."[2] Though there is no parallel constitutional provision expressly prohibiting the federal government from denying equal protection of the law, the Supreme Court has held that equal protection principles similarly apply to the federal government.[3] Under the Constitution's equal protection guarantees, when courts review governmental action that distinguishes between classes of people, they apply different levels of scrutiny depending on the classification involved. The more suspect the government's classification, or the more likely that the government's classification was motivated by discrimination, the higher the level of scrutiny that courts will utilize in evaluating the government's action.[4] Increased scrutiny raises the likelihood that a court will find the action unconstitutional. Generally speaking, there are three such levels of scrutiny: (1) strict scrutiny; (2) intermediate scrutiny; and (3) rational basis review.

Strict scrutiny is the most demanding form of judicial review. The Supreme Court has observed that strict scrutiny applies to governmental classifications that are constitutionally "suspect," or that interfere with fundamental rights.[5] In determining whether a classification is suspect, courts consider whether the classified group (1) has historically been subject to discrimination; (2) is a minority group exhibiting an unchangeable characteristic that establishes the group as distinct; or (3) is inadequately protected by the political process.[6] There are generally three governmental classifications that are suspect—those based on race, national origin, and alienage.[7] When applying strict scrutiny to governmental action, reviewing courts consider whether the governmental action is *narrowly tailored* to a *compelling* government interest.[8] The government bears the burden of proving the constitutional validity of its action under strict scrutiny, and, in doing so, must generally show that it cannot meet its goals via less discriminatory means.[9]

Intermediate scrutiny is less searching than strict scrutiny, though it subjects governmental action to more stringent inspection than rational basis review. Intermediate scrutiny applies to "quasi-suspect" classifications such as classifications based on gender[10] or illegitimacy.[11] When reviewing courts apply intermediate scrutiny to governmental action, they determine whether the action is *substantially related* to achieving an *important* government interest.[12] As with strict scrutiny, the government bears the burden of establishing the constitutional validity of its actions under intermediate scrutiny.[13]

Rational basis review is the least searching form of judicial scrutiny, and generally applies to all classifications that are not subject to heightened levels of scrutiny.[14] For governmental action to survive rational basis review, it must be *rationally* related to a *legitimate* government interest.[15] When evaluating governmental action under rational basis review, courts consider the legitimacy of any possible governmental purpose behind the action.[16] That is, courts are not limited to considering the actual purposes behind the government's action.[17]

Additionally, the governmental action needs only be a reasonable way of achieving a legitimate government purpose to survive rational basis review; it does not need to be the most reasonable way of doing so, or even more reasonable than alternatives.[18] Accordingly, rational basis review is deferential to the government, and courts generally presume that governmental action that is subject to such review is constitutionally valid.[19] Parties challenging governmental actions bear the burden of establishing their invalidity under rational basis review.[20]

Substantive due Process

The U.S. Constitution's due process guarantees are contained within two separate clauses; one can be found in the Fifth Amendment, and the other resides in the Fourteenth Amendment. Each clause provides that the government shall not deprive a person of "life, liberty, or property, without due process of law."[21] However, the Fifth Amendment applies to action by the federal government, whereas the Fourteenth Amendment applies to state action.[22]

The Constitution's due process language makes clear that the government cannot deprive individuals of life, liberty, or property without observing certain procedural requirements. The Supreme Court has interpreted this language to also include substantive guarantees that prohibit the government from taking action that unduly burdens certain liberty interests.[23] More specifically, substantive due process protects against undue governmental infringement upon fundamental rights.[24] In determining whether a right is fundamental, Supreme Court precedent looks to whether the right was historically and traditionally recognized, and whether failing to recognize the right would contravene liberty and justice.[25]

The Supreme Court has held that governmental action infringing upon fundamental rights is subject to strict scrutiny,[26] and thus must be *narrowly tailored* to a *compelling* government interest.[27] Under strict scrutiny, the government must generally show that it has a "substantial" and "legitimate" need for its action to be in furtherance of a compelling government interest.[28] If the government successfully establishes a compelling interest, its action cannot encumber fundamental rights any more than is necessary to achieve the government's need.[29] Additionally, the government could not have possibly taken alternative action that would similarly further its interest while being less burdensome on fundamental rights.[30] Otherwise, the government's action is not narrowly tailored to the government's interest.[31] The Supreme Court has recognized a number of rights as fundamental, including the right to have children,[32] use contraception,[33] and marry.[34]

In *Obergefell*, the Court considered whether the Fourteenth Amendment's substantive due process guarantees require states to issue marriage licenses to same-sex couples and require states to recognize same-sex marriages that were legally formed in other states.

The Supreme Court Invalidates State Same-Sex Marriage Bans in *Obergefell*

The Supreme Court resolved a circuit split on the constitutionality of state same-sex marriage bans, finding them unconstitutional in *Obergefell v. Hodges*. In doing so, the Court relied on the Constitution's due process and equal protection principles to hold that states must issue marriage licenses to same-sex couples and recognize same-sex marriages that were legally formed in other states.

The majority in *Obergefell* rested its decision upon the fundamental right to marry. The Court observed that it has long found the right to marry to be constitutionally protected, though it acknowledged that its precedent describing the right presumed an opposite-sex relationship.[35] Even so, according to the Court, these cases have identified reasons why the right to marry is fundamental,[36] which apply equally to same-sex couples. [37] These reasons included (1) personal choice in whom to marry is inherent in the concept of individual autonomy; (2) marriage's unique support and recognition of a two-person, committed union; (3) the safeguarding of children within a marriage, as both same-sex couples and opposite-sex couples have children; and (4) marriage as a keystone of the nation's social order, with no distinction between same-sex couples and opposite-sex couples in states conferring benefits and responsibilities upon marriages.[38] Accordingly, the Court extended the fundamental right to marry to same-sex couples.

In holding that the fundamental right to marry includes same-sex couples' right to marry, the Court appeared to acknowledge its departure from precedent for determining whether a right is fundamental—mentioned earlier in this report—which considers whether it is "deeply rooted in this Nation's history and tradition and implicit in the concept of ordered liberty."[39] The Court observed that if rights were defined by who could historically use them, old practices could continuously prevent new groups from exercising fundamental rights.[40] As such, the Court found that "rights come not from ancient sources alone. They rise, too, from a better informed understanding of how constitutional imperatives define a liberty that remains urgent in our own era."[41]

After determining that the fundamental right to marry includes the right of same-sex couples to marry, the Court also seemed to depart from precedent—and the approaches of courts of appeals that relied on the fundamental right to marry to strike down state same-sex marriage bans—by not applying strict scrutiny to such bans. As previously noted, courts generally subject governmental action that infringes upon a fundamental right to strict scrutiny, requiring that the action be narrowly tailored to a compelling government interest to be constitutional.[42] The states had argued two primary interests for their bans on same-marriage: (1) the desire to wait and see how the same-sex marriage debate progresses before changing long-existing marriage norms; and (2) incentivizing procreating couples to stay together during child rearing. However, the Court made no mention of whether the state same-sex marriage bans at issue were narrowly tailored to these justifications. Rather, the Court noted why these justifications were invalid without appearing to apply any of the typical levels of judicial review (i.e., rational basis review, intermediate scrutiny, or strict scrutiny).[43]

The Court held that both equal protection and due process guarantees protect the fundamental right to marry, and that states can no longer deny this right to same-sex couples.[44] Importantly, in doing so, the Court did not hold that classifications based on sexual orientation warrant any form of heightened scrutiny. In fact, the Court made no mention of the proper level of scrutiny applicable to such classifications.

Some of the dissenting Justices in *Obergefell* thought that the majority exceeded the Court's proper role by removing the question of whether same-sex couples have the right to marry from the democratic process, where, they stated, it is properly resolved.[45] According to these Justices, the five-person majority should not have resolved the hotly contested issue of same-sex marriage for the entire country; such resolution should have come from the people.[46] The dissenting Justices also voiced concern with the majority looking beyond history and tradition to establish a fundamental right contrary to Supreme Court precedent.[47] According to the dissenting Justices, the requirement that fundamental rights be rooted in tradition and history exists to prevent the Court from imparting its policy decisions regarding which rights have constitutional protection.[48]

IMPLICATIONS OF THE SUPREME COURT'S DECISION IN *OBERGEFELL*

Although the Supreme Court answered questions surrounding the constitutionality of state same-sex marriage bans in *Obergefell*, its decision raised a number of other questions. These include questions regarding, among other things, *Obergefell*'s broader impact on the rights of gay individuals; the proper level of judicial scrutiny applicable to classifications based on sexual orientation; what the decision might mean for laws prohibiting plural marriages; the Court's approach to recognizing fundamental rights moving forward; and the proper level of judicial scrutiny applicable to governmental action interfering with fundamental rights. This section briefly explores these questions.

Obergefell raised questions about the decision's broader impact on the rights of gay individuals— that is, whether its rationale extends rights to gay individuals outside of the marriage context. However, the decision appears limited to the marriage context. Although the majority opinion did make reference to same-sex marriage bans implicating equal protection guarantees, its holding rested entirely on such bans infringing upon the fundamental right to marry in violation of both equal protection and due process guarantees. The Court did not mention whether classifications based on sexual orientation are suspect or quasi-suspect, and thus warrant any form of heightened scrutiny. If the Court had rendered such a holding, its decision would have arguably had broader implications for the rights of gay individuals, as it would have potentially subjected all governmental action that classifies based on sexual orientation to a heightened form of judicial scrutiny.

Prior to *Obergefell*, federal appeals courts were split regarding the proper level of judicial scrutiny applicable to governmental action that classifies based on sexual orientation. The U.S. Court of Appeals for the Ninth Circuit (Ninth Circuit) has held that classifications based on sexual orientation warrant heightened scrutiny, though it did not clarify whether this heightened scrutiny was intermediate or strict scrutiny.[49] The U.S. Court of Appeals for the Second Circuit (Second Circuit) has similarly found that classifications based on sexual orientation are quasi-suspect, and thus any governmental action that classifies based on sexual orientation is subject to intermediate scrutiny.[50] Conversely, however, the U.S. Court of Appeals for the Sixth Circuit (Sixth Circuit) has held that governmental action that classifies based on sexual orientation is neither suspect nor quasi-suspect, and thus subject only to rational basis review.[51]

Because the Court's decision in *Obergefell* rested on the fundamental right to marry—and therefore seems limited to the marriage context—nothing in the opinion appears to resolve the circuit split between the Second, Sixth, and Ninth Circuits regarding the correct level of scrutiny applicable to classifications based on sexual orientation. Other lower courts will be left to grapple with this issue in the future. This ambiguity leaves open the possibility that, moving forward, circuit courts could either, like the Second and Ninth Circuits, apply heightened scrutiny to laws that classify based on sexual orientation (e.g., laws that provide exemptions from antidiscrimination legislation for religious entities based on their objections to certain sexual orientations), or could apply rational basis review to such laws like the Sixth Circuit. The fact that some lower courts may apply heightened scrutiny to government action that classifies based on sexual orientation where other courts may not is significant because, as discussed earlier in this report, laws subject to higher levels of scrutiny are more likely to be found unconstitutional. As such, this could create a situation wherein similar laws that classify based on sexual orientation receive dissimilar outcomes when facing constitutional challenge, depending on the evaluating court.

The Supreme Court's decision in *Obergefell* also raised questions regarding whether the Court's rationale could potentially extend the fundamental right to marry to polygamy. In fact, Chief Justice John Roberts, in his dissent in *Obergefell*, seems to suggest that the majority's opinion could lead to the legalization of plural marriages.[52] However, the majority's opinion seems crafted so as to try to limit its reach to the same-sex marriage context, in a possible attempt to prevent its rationale from extending the fundamental right to marry to plural marriages.

As previously discussed, the majority in *Obergefell* found that the four reasons why the right to marry is fundamental apply equally to same-sex couples, and thus extended the fundamental right to marry to same-sex couples. Some commentators have observed that there are distinctions between plural marriages and same-sex marriages sufficient to prevent *Obergefell*'s rationale from being extended to legalize plural marriage.[53] Conversely, other commentators have observed that parts of the Court's opinion discussing why the fundamental right to marry includes same-sex marriage (e.g., the majority's consideration of individual autonomy and family) could potentially provide basis for extending constitutional protections to plural marriages.[54]

Additionally, the majority in *Obergefell* seemingly departed from precedent for determining whether a right is fundamental by looking beyond historical and traditional recognition. This deviation from prior cases raises the possibility that, when determining whether a right is fundamental in the future, the Court will consider how the right is viewed at the time, in addition to its historical and traditional recognition. This could have the effect of expanding the number of rights that are deemed fundamental for purposes of substantive due process protections.

Finally, the Court did not clarify which, if any, of the typical levels of judicial review (i.e., rational basis review, intermediate scrutiny, or strict scrutiny) it applied to state same-sex marriage bans after finding that such bans interfere with same-sex couples' fundamental right to marry. Moving forward, this raises questions regarding the proper level of judicial scrutiny applicable to governmental action that infringes upon fundamental rights. Given that increased scrutiny decreases the likelihood that a court will find government action constitutional, this could create ambiguity regarding the degree to which the government can permissibly take action that interferes with fundamental rights.

End Notes

[1] Previously, the Fourth, Seventh, Ninth, and Tenth Circuits had struck down state same-sex marriage bans under equal protection or due process grounds after generally, though not uniformly, subjecting them to heightened levels of judicial scrutiny. Bostic v. Schaeffer, 760 F.3d 352 (4th Cir. 2014); Baskin v. Bogan, 766 F.3d 648 (7th Cir. 2014); Latta v. Otter, 771 F.3d 456 (9th Cir. 2014); Bishop v. Smith, 760 F.3d 1070 (10th Cir. 2014); Kitchen v. Herbert, 755 F.3d 1193 (10th Cir. 2014). Conversely, the Sixth Circuit had upheld state same-sex marriage bans and observed that such bans warrant the lowest level of judicial review. DeBoer v. Snyder, 772 F.3d 388 (6th Cir. 2014).

[2] U.S. Const. amend. XIV, §1.

[3] *See* Bolling v. Sharpe, 347 U.S. 497 (1954). More specifically, the Court has held that the Fifth Amendment's guarantee of "due process of the law," applicable to the federal government, incorporates equal protection guarantees. *See id.* at 500.

[4] *Compare* City of Cleburne v. Cleburne Living Center, 473 U.S. 432 (1985) (holding that mental disability is not a "quasi-suspect" classification, and thus is entitled to rational basis review), *with* Graham v. Richardson, 403 U.S. 365 (1971) (holding that classifications based on alienage are "inherently suspect," and are subject to strict scrutiny).

[5] *See* Mass. Bd. of Retirement v. Murgia, 427 U.S. 307, 312 (1976); *see also* Heller v. Doe, 509 U.S. 312, 319 (1993).

[6] *See* Lyng v. Castillo, 477 U.S. 635, 638 (1986); *see also* United States v. Carolene Prods. Co., 304 U.S. 144, 152 n. 4 (1938).

[7] Graham, 403 U.S. at 371-72 ("... the Court's decisions have established that classifications based on alienage, like those based on nationality or race, are inherently suspect and subject to close judicial scrutiny.").

[8] Parents Involved in Cmty. Schs. v. Seattle Sch. Dist. No. 1, 551 U.S. 701, 720 (2007).

[9] *See* Fisher v. University of Tex. at Austin, 133 S. Ct. 2411, 2420 (2014).

[10] United States v. Virginia, 518 U.S. 515, 533 (1996); *see* Miss. Univ. for Women v. Hogan, 458 U.S. 718, 724 (1982).

[11] Clark v. Jeter, 486 U.S. 456, 461 (1988) ("Between these extremes of rational basis review and strict scrutiny lies a level of intermediate scrutiny, which generally has been applied to discriminatory classifications based on sex or illegitimacy.").

[12] *See* Craig v. Boren, 429 U.S. 190, 198 (1976); *see also Clark*, 486 U.S. at 461.

[13] *Virginia*, 518 U.S. at 533; *see Miss. Univ. for Women*, 458 U.S. at 724.

[14] *See Cleburne Living Center*, 473 U.S at 440-42; *see also* Schweiker v. Wilson, 450 U.S. 221, 230 (1981).

[15] *See City of Cleburne*, 473 U.S. at 440.

[16] *See* Nordlinger v. Hahn, 505 U.S. 1, 15 (1992); *see also Heller*, 509 U.S. at 320.

[17] *See Nordlinger*, 505 U.S. at 15; *see also Heller*, 509 U.S. at 320.

[18] *See Schweiker*, 450 U.S. 221, 235 (1981) (observing that, under rational basis review, "[a]s long as the classificatory scheme chosen by Congress rationally advances a reasonable and identifiable governmental objective, we must disregard the existence of other methods of allocation that we, as individuals, perhaps would have preferred."); *see also Heller*, 509 U.S. at 320 (observing that under rational basis review, "a classification 'must be upheld against equal protection challenge if there is any reasonably conceivable state of facts that could provide a rational basis for the classification.'") (quoting F.C.C. v. Beach Commc'ns, Inc., 508 U.S. 307, 312 (1993)).

[19] *See Beach Commc'ns, Inc.*, 508 U.S. at 315; *see also Murgia*, 427 U.S. at 315.

[20] *Heller*, 509 U.S. at 320 (noting that, when reviewing a governmental classification under rational basis review, a governmental action is "presumed constitutional," and the burden lies on the party attacking the governmental action to establish the action's unconstitutionality.).

[21] U.S. Const. amend. XIV, §1; U.S. Const. amend. V.

[22] *See* U.S. Const. amend. XIV, §1; U.S. Const. amend. V.

[23] *See* Washington v. Glucksberg, 521 U.S. 702, 719-720 (1997).

[24] *See id.*

[25] *See id.* at 720.

[26] *See* Reno v. Flores, 507 U.S. 292, 301-02 (1993).

[27] *Id.* (observing that a line of Supreme Court cases interprets the Fifth Amendment's and Fourteenth Amendment's due process principles to "forbid[] the government to infringe certain 'fundamental' liberty interests *at all* ... unless the infringement is narrowly tailored to serve a compelling state interest.").

[28] San Antonio Indep. School Dist. v. Rodriguez, 411 U.S. 1, 98 (1973).

[29] *See* Dunn v. Blumstein, 405 U.S. 330, 343 (1972).

[30] *Id.* ("if there are other, reasonable ways to achieve [government interests] with a lesser burden on constitutionally protected activity, a State may not choose the way of greater interference. If it acts at all, it must choose 'less drastic means.'") (quoting Shelton v. Tucker, 364 U.S. 479, 488 (1960)).

[31] *See id.*

[32] Skinner v. Okla., 316 U.S. 535 (1942).

[33] Griswold v. Connecticut, 381 U.S. 479 (1965).

[34] Loving v. Virginia, 388 U.S. 1 (1967).

[35] *Obergefell*, 135 S.Ct. at 2598.

[36] *Id.*

[37] *Id.* at 2599.

[38] *Id.* at 2599-2601.

[39] *Glucksberg*, 512 U.S. at 720.

[40] *Obergefell*, 135 S. Ct. at 2602 ("If rights were defined by who exercised them in the past, then received practices could serve as their own continued justification and new groups could not invoke rights once denied.").

[41] *Id.*

[42] *See Flores*, 507 U.S. at 301-02.

[43] *See Obergefell,* 135 S. Ct. at 2605-07.

[44] *Id.* at 2604.

[45] *Id.* at 2612, 2615 (Roberts, J., dissenting).

[46] *See id.*

[47] *See id.* at 2617.

[48] *See id.*

[49] *See Latta*, 771 F.3d at 468.

[50] Windsor v. United States, 699 F.3d 169, 185 (2nd Cir. 2012).

[51] Davis v. Prison Health Servs., 679 F.3d 433, 438 (6th Cir. 2012).

[52] *See Obergefell*, 135 S. Ct. at 2621 ("It is striking how much of the majority's reasoning would apply with equal force to the claim of a fundamental right to plural marriage.").

[53] *See, e.g.*, Joanna L. Grossman and Lawrence M. Friedman, *Is Three Still a Crowd? Polygamy and the Law After Obergefell v. Hodges*, JUSTIA, July 7, 2015, https://verdict.justia.com/2015/07/07/is-three-still-a-crowd-polygamy-andthe-law-after-obergefell-v-hodges (observing that, to win in court, polygamists must "convince a court that the justification for allowing same-sex couples to marry applies with equal force to a person who wants multiple spouses," and questioning whether the four "main reasons for recognizing the right of same-sex couples to marry" apply to polygamists); *see also* Richard A. Posner, *The Chief Justice's Dissent is Heartless*, Slate, June 27, 2015, http://www.slate.com/articles/news_and_politics/the_breakfast_table/features/ 2015/ scotus_roundup/ supreme_court _gay_marriage_john _roberts_dissent_in_ obergefell_ is_ heartless.html.

[54] *See, e.g.*, William Baude, *Is Polygamy Next?*, N. Y. TIMES, July 21, 2015, http://www.nytimes.com/2015/07/21/ opinion/is-polygamy-next.html?mabR eward= CTM &action= click&pgtype=Homepage&region=CColumn&module= Recommendation&src=rechp&WT.nav=RecEngine; *see also* Jonathan Turley, *The Trouble with the 'Dignity' of Same-Sex Marriage*, Wash. Post, July 2, 2015, https://www.washingtonpost.com/opinions/the-trouble-with-the-dignity-ofsame-sex-marriage/2015/07/02/43bd8f70-1f4e-11e5-aeb9-a411a84c9d55_story.html.

In: The Legalization of Same-Sex Marriage ISBN: 978-1-63483-942-6
Editor: Kendra Vasquez

Chapter 4

DECISION OF THE SUPREME COURT OF THE UNITED STATES IN THE CASE OF OBERGEFELL ET AL. V. HODGES, DIRECTOR, OHIO DEPARTMENT OF HEALTH, ET AL.*

(Slip Opinion) OCTOBER TERM, 20141

Syllabus

NOTE: Where it is feasible, a syllabus (headnote) will be released, as is being done in connection with this case, at the time the opinion is issued. The syllabus constitutes no part of the opinion of the Court but has been prepared by the Reporter of Decisions for the convenience of the reader. See *United States* v. *Detroit Timber & Lumber Co.,* 200 U. S. 321, 337.

SUPREME COURT OF THE UNITED STATES

Syllabus

OBERGEFELL ET AL. *v.* HODGES, DIRECTOR, OHIO DEPARTMENT OF HEALTH, ET AL.

---

* This is an edited, reformatted and augmented version of the official slip opinion as delivered by the U.S. Supreme Court on June 26, 2015.

CERTIORARI TO THE UNITED STATES COURT OF APPEALS FOR THE SIXTH CIRCUIT

No. 14–556. Argued April 28, 2015—Decided June 26, 2015[†]

Michigan, Kentucky, Ohio, and Tennessee define marriage as a union between one man and one woman. The petitioners, 14 same-sex couples and two men whose same-sex partners are deceased, filed suits in Federal District Courts in their home States, claiming that respondent state officials violate the Fourteenth Amendment by denying them the right to marry or to have marriages lawfully performed in another State given full recognition. Each District Court ruled in petitioners' favor, but the Sixth Circuit consolidated the cases and reversed.

Held: The Fourteenth Amendment requires a State to license a marriage between two people of the same sex and to recognize a marriage between two people of the same sex when their marriage was lawfully licensed and performed out-of-State. Pp. 3–28.

(a) Before turning to the governing principles and precedents, it is appropriate to note the history of the subject now before the Court. Pp. 3–10.

(1) The history of marriage as a union between two persons of the opposite sex marks the beginning of these cases. To the respondents, it would demean a timeless institution if marriage were extended to same-sex couples. But the petitioners, far from seeking to devalue marriage, seek it for themselves because of their respect—and need—for its privileges and responsibilities, as illustrated by the petitioners' own experiences. Pp. 3–6.

(2) The history of marriage is one of both continuity and change. Changes, such as the decline of arranged marriages and the abandonment of the law of coverture, have worked deep transformations in the structure of marriage, affecting aspects of marriage once viewed as essential. These new insights have strengthened, not weakened, the institution. Changed understandings of marriage are characteristic of a Nation where new dimensions of freedom become apparent to new generations.

This dynamic can be seen in the Nation's experience with gay and lesbian rights. Well into the 20th century, many States condemned same-sex intimacy as immoral, and homosexuality was treated as an illness. Later in the century,

---

[†] Together with No. 14–562, Tanco et al. v. Haslam, Governor of Tennessee, et al., No. 14–571, DeBoer et al. v. Snyder, Governor of Michigan, et al., and No. 14–574, Bourke et al. v. Beshear, Governor of Kentucky, also on certiorari to the same court.

cultural and political developments allowed same-sex couples to lead more open and public lives. Extensive public and private dialogue followed, along with shifts in public attitudes. Questions about the legal treatment of gays and lesbians soon reached the courts, where they could be discussed in the formal discourse of the law. In 2003, this Court overruled its 1986 decision in *Bowers* v. *Hardwick*, 478 U. S. 186, which upheld a Georgia law that criminalized certain homosexual acts, concluding laws making same-sex intimacy a crime "demea[n] the lives of homosexual persons." *Lawrence* v. *Texas*, 539 U. S. 558, 575. In 2012, the federal Defense of Marriage Act was also struck down. *United States* v. *Windsor*, 570 U. S. ___. Numerous same-sex marriage cases reaching the federal courts and state supreme courts have added to the dialogue. Pp. 6– 10.

(b) The Fourteenth Amendment requires a State to license a marriage between two people of the same sex. Pp. 10–27.

(1) The fundamental liberties protected by the Fourteenth Amendment's Due Process Clause extend to certain personal choices central to individual dignity and autonomy, including intimate choices defining personal identity and beliefs. See, *e.g., Eisenstadt* v. *Baird*, 405 U. S. 438, 453; *Griswold* v. *Connecticut*, 381 U. S. 479, 484–486. Courts must exercise reasoned judgment in identifying interests of the person so fundamental that the State must accord them its respect. History and tradition guide and discipline the inquiry but do not set its outer boundaries. When new insight reveals discord between the Constitution's central protections and a received legal stricture, a claim to liberty must be addressed.

Applying these tenets, the Court has long held the right to marry is protected by the Constitution. For example, *Loving* v. *Virginia*, 388 U. S. 1, 12, invalidated bans on interracial unions, and *Turner* v. *Safley*, 482 U. S. 78, 95, held that prisoners could not be denied the right to marry. To be sure, these cases presumed a relationship involving opposite-sex partners, as did *Baker* v. *Nelson*, 409 U. S. 810, a one-line summary decision issued in 1972, holding that the exclusion of same-sex couples from marriage did not present a substantial federal question. But other, more instructive precedents have expressed broader principles. See, *e.g., Lawrence, supra,* at 574. In assessing whether the force and rationale of its cases apply to same-sex couples, the Court must respect the basic reasons why the right to marry has been long protected. See, *e.g., Eisenstadt, supra*, at 453–454. This analysis compels the conclusion that same-sex couples may exercise the right to marry. Pp. 10–12.

(2) Four principles and traditions demonstrate that the reasons marriage is fundamental under the Constitution apply with equal force to same-sex

couples. The first premise of this Court's relevant precedents is that the right to personal choice regarding marriage is inherent in the concept of individual autonomy. This abiding connection between marriage and liberty is why *Loving* invalidated interracial marriage bans under the Due Process Clause. See 388 U. S., at 12. Decisions about marriage are among the most intimate that an individual can make. See *Lawrence*, *supra*, at 574. This is true for all persons, whatever their sexual orientation.

A second principle in this Court's jurisprudence is that the right to marry is fundamental because it supports a two-person union unlike any other in its importance to the committed individuals. The intimate association protected by this right was central to *Griswold* v. *Connecticut*, which held the Constitution protects the right of married couples to use contraception, 381 U. S., at 485, and was acknowledged in *Turner*, *supra,* at 95. Same-sex couples have the same right as opposite-sex couples to enjoy intimate association, a right extending beyond mere freedom from laws making same-sex intimacy a criminal offense. See *Lawrence, supra*, at 567.

A third basis for protecting the right to marry is that it safeguards children and families and thus draws meaning from related rights of childrearing, procreation, and education. See, *e.g., Pierce* v. *Society of Sisters*, 268 U. S. 510. Without the recognition, stability, and predictability marriage offers, children suffer the stigma of knowing their families are somehow lesser. They also suffer the significant material costs of being raised by unmarried parents, relegated to a more difficult and uncertain family life. The marriage laws at issue thus harm and humiliate the children of same-sex couples. See *Windsor*, *supra,* at ___. This does not mean that the right to marry is less meaningful for those who do not or cannot have children. Precedent protects the right of a married couple not to procreate, so the right to marry cannot be conditioned on the capacity or commitment to procreate.

Finally, this Court's cases and the Nation's traditions make clear that marriage is a keystone of the Nation's social order. See *Maynard* v. *Hill*, 125 U. S. 190, 211. States have contributed to the fundamental character of marriage by placing it at the center of many facets of the legal and social order. There is no difference between same- and opposite-sex couples with respect to this principle, yet same-sex couples are denied the constellation of benefits that the States have linked to marriage and are consigned to an instability many opposite-sex couples would find intolerable. It is demeaning to lock same-sex couples out of a central institution of the Nation's society, for they too may aspire to the transcendent purposes of marriage.

The limitation of marriage to opposite-sex couples may long have seemed natural and just, but its inconsistency with the central meaning of the fundamental right to marry is now manifest. Pp. 12–18.

(3) The right of same-sex couples to marry is also derived from the Fourteenth Amendment's guarantee of equal protection. The Due Process Clause and the Equal Protection Clause are connected in a profound way. Rights implicit in liberty and rights secured by equal protection may rest on different precepts and are not always coextensive, yet each may be instructive as to the meaning and reach of the other. This dynamic is reflected in *Loving,* where the Court invoked both the Equal Protection Clause and the Due Process Clause; and in *Zablocki* v. *Redhail*, 434 U. S. 374, where the Court invalidated a law barring fathers delinquent on child-support payments from marrying. Indeed, recognizing that new insights and societal understandings can reveal unjustified inequality within fundamental institutions that once passed unnoticed and unchallenged, this Court has invoked equal protection principles to invalidate laws imposing sex-based inequality on marriage, see, *e.g., Kirchberg* v. *Feenstra*, 450 U. S. 455, 460–461, and confirmed the relation between liberty and equality, see, *e.g., M. L. B.* v. *S. L. J.*, 519 U. S. 102, 120–121.

The Court has acknowledged the interlocking nature of these constitutional safeguards in the context of the legal treatment of gays and lesbians. See *Lawrence*, 539 U. S., at 575. This dynamic also applies to same-sex marriage. The challenged laws burden the liberty of same-sex couples, and they abridge central precepts of equality. The marriage laws at issue are in essence unequal: Same-sex couples are denied benefits afforded opposite-sex couples and are barred from exercising a fundamental right. Especially against a long history of disapproval of their relationships, this denial works a grave and continuing harm, serving to disrespect and subordinate gays and lesbians. Pp. 18–22.

(4) The right to marry is a fundamental right inherent in the liberty of the person, and under the Due Process and Equal Protection Clauses of the Fourteenth Amendment couples of the same-sex may not be deprived of that right and that liberty. Same-sex couples may exercise the fundamental right to marry. *Baker* v. *Nelson* is overruled. The State laws challenged by the petitioners in these cases are held invalid to the extent they exclude same-sex couples from civil marriage on the same terms and conditions as opposite-sex couples. Pp. 22–23.

(5) There may be an initial inclination to await further legislation, litigation, and debate, but referenda, legislative debates, and grassroots

campaigns; studies and other writings; and extensive litigation in state and federal courts have led to an enhanced understanding of the issue. While the Constitution contemplates that democracy is the appropriate process for change, individuals who are harmed need not await legislative action before asserting a fundamental right. *Bowers,* in effect, upheld state action that denied gays and lesbians a fundamental right. Though it was eventually repudiated, men and women suffered pain and humiliation in the interim, and the effects of these injuries no doubt lingered long after *Bowers* was overruled. A ruling against same-sex couples would have the same effect and would be unjustified under the Fourteenth Amendment. The petitioners' stories show the urgency of the issue they present to the Court, which has a duty to address these claims and answer these questions. Respondents' argument that allowing same-sex couples to wed will harm marriage as an institution rests on a counterintuitive view of opposite-sex couples' decisions about marriage and parenthood. Finally, the First Amendment ensures that religions, those who adhere to religious doctrines, and others have protection as they seek to teach the principles that are so fulfilling and so central to their lives and faiths. Pp. 23–27.

(c) The Fourteenth Amendment requires States to recognize same-sex marriages validly performed out of State. Since same-sex couples may now exercise the fundamental right to marry in all States, there is no lawful basis for a State to refuse to recognize a lawful same-sex marriage performed in another State on the ground of its same-sex character. Pp. 27–28.

772 F. 3d 388, reversed.

KENNEDY, J., delivered the opinion of the Court, in which GINSBURG, BREYER, SOTOMAYOR, and KAGAN, JJ., joined. ROBERTS, C. J., filed a dissenting opinion, in which SCALIA and THOMAS, JJ., joined. SCALIA, J., filed a dissenting opinion, in which THOMAS, J., joined. THOMAS, J., filed a dissenting opinion, in which SCALIA, J., joined. ALITO, J., filed a dissenting opinion, in which SCALIA and THOMAS, JJ., joined.

OPINION OF THE COURT

NOTICE: This opinion is subject to formal revision before publication in the preliminary print of the United States Reports. Readers are requested to notify the Reporter of Decisions, Supreme Court of the United States, Washington, D. C. 20543, of any typographical or other formal errors, in order that corrections may be made before the preliminary print goes to press.

SUPREME COURT OF THE UNITED STATES

Nos. 14–556, 14-562, 14-571 and 14–574
JAMES OBERGEFELL, ET AL., PETITIONERS
14–556 *v.*
RICHARD HODGES, DIRECTOR, OHIO
DEPARTMENT OF HEALTH, ET AL.;
VALERIA TANCO, ET AL., PETITIONERS
14–562 *v.*
BILL HASLAM, GOVERNOR OF
TENNESSEE, ET AL.;
APRIL DEBOER, ET AL., PETITIONERS
14–571 *v.*
RICK SNYDER, GOVERNOR OF MICHIGAN,
ET AL.; AND
GREGORY BOURKE, ET AL., PETITIONERS
14–574 *v.*
STEVE BESHEAR, GOVERNOR OF
KENTUCKY
ON WRITS OF CERTIORARI TO THE UNITED STATES COURT OF
APPEALS FOR THE SIXTH CIRCUIT
[June 26, 2015]

JUSTICE KENNEDY delivered the opinion of the Court.

The Constitution promises liberty to all within its reach, a liberty that includes certain specific rights that allow persons, within a lawful realm, to define and express their identity. The petitioners in these cases seek to find that liberty by marrying someone of the same sex and having their marriages deemed lawful on the same terms and conditions as marriages between persons of the opposite sex.

I

These cases come from Michigan, Kentucky, Ohio, and Tennessee, States that define marriage as a union between one man and one woman. See, *e.g.,* Mich. Const., Art. I, §25; Ky. Const. §233A; Ohio Rev. Code Ann. §3101.01 (Lexis 2008); Tenn. Const., Art. XI, §18. The petitioners are 14 same-sex couples and two men whose same-sex partners are deceased. The respondents are state officials responsible for enforcing the laws in question. The petitioners claim the respondents violate the Fourteenth Amendment by denying them the right to marry or to have their marriages, lawfully performed in another State, given full recognition.

Petitioners filed these suits in United States District Courts in their home States. Each District Court ruled in their favor. Citations to those cases are in Appendix A, *infra*. The respondents appealed the decisions against them to the United States Court of Appeals for the Sixth Circuit. It consolidated the cases and reversed the judgments of the District Courts. *DeBoer* v. *Snyder*, 772 F. 3d 388 (2014). The Court of Appeals held that a State has no constitutional obligation to license same-sex marriages or to recognize same-sex marriages performed out of State.

The petitioners sought certiorari. This Court granted review, limited to two questions. 574 U. S. ___ (2015). The first, presented by the cases from Michigan and Kentucky, is whether the Fourteenth Amendment requires a State to license a marriage between two people of the same sex. The second, presented by the cases from Ohio, Tennessee, and, again, Kentucky, is whether the Fourteenth Amendment requires a State to recognize a same-sex marriage licensed and performed in a State which does grant that right.

II

Before addressing the principles and precedents that govern these cases, it is appropriate to note the history of the subject now before the Court.

A

From their beginning to their most recent page, the annals of human history reveal the transcendent importance of marriage. The lifelong union of a man and a woman always has promised nobility and dignity to all persons, without regard to their station in life. Marriage is sacred to those who live by their religions and offers unique fulfillment to those who find meaning in the secular realm. Its dynamic allows two people to find a life that could not be found alone, for a marriage becomes greater than just the two persons. Rising from the most basic human needs, marriage is essential to our most profound hopes and aspirations.

The centrality of marriage to the human condition makes it unsurprising that the institution has existed for millennia and across civilizations. Since the dawn of history, marriage has transformed strangers into relatives, binding families and societies together. Confucius taught that marriage lies at the foundation of government. 2 Li Chi: Book of Rites 266 (C. Chai & W. Chai eds., J. Legge transl. 1967). This wisdom was echoed centuries later and half a world away by Cicero, who wrote, “The first bond of society is marriage; next, children; and then the family.” See De Officiis 57 (W. Miller transl. 1913). There are untold references to the beauty of marriage in religious and philosophical texts spanning time, cultures, and faiths, as well as in art and literature in all their forms. It is fair and necessary to say these references were based on the understanding that marriage is a union between two persons of the opposite sex.

That history is the beginning of these cases. The respondents say it should be the end as well. To them, it would demean a timeless institution if the concept and lawful status of marriage were extended to two persons of the same sex. Marriage, in their view, is by its nature a gender-differentiated union of man and woman. This view long has been held—and continues to be held—in good faith by reasonable and sincere people here and throughout the world.

The petitioners acknowledge this history but contend that these cases cannot end there. Were their intent to demean the revered idea and reality of marriage, the petitioners’ claims would be of a different order. But that is neither their purpose nor their submission. To the contrary, it is the enduring importance of marriage that underlies the petitioners’ contentions. This, they say, is their whole point. Far from seeking to devalue marriage, the petitioners seek it for themselves because of their respect—and need—for its privileges and responsibilities. And their immutable nature dictates that same-sex marriage is their only real path to this profound commitment.

Recounting the circumstances of three of these cases illustrates the urgency of the petitioners’ cause from their perspective. Petitioner James Obergefell, a plaintiff in the Ohio case, met John Arthur over two decades ago. They fell in love and started a life together, establishing a lasting, committed relation. In 2011, however, Arthur was diagnosed with amyotrophic lateral sclerosis, or ALS. This debilitating disease is progressive, with no known cure. Two years ago, Obergefell and Arthur decided to commit to one another, resolving to marry before Arthur died. To fulfill their mutual promise, they traveled from Ohio to Maryland, where same-sex marriage was legal. It was difficult for Arthur to move, and so the couple were wed inside a medical transport plane as it remained on the tarmac in Baltimore. Three months later, Arthur died. Ohio law does not permit Obergefell to be listed as the surviving spouse on Arthur's death certificate. By statute, they must remain strangers even in death, a state-imposed separation Obergefell deems "hurtful for the rest of time." App. in No. 14–556 etc., p. 38. He brought suit to be shown as the surviving spouse on Arthur's death certificate.

April DeBoer and Jayne Rowse are co-plaintiffs in the case from Michigan. They celebrated a commitment ceremony to honor their permanent relation in 2007. They both work as nurses, DeBoer in a neonatal unit and Rowse in an emergency unit. In 2009, DeBoer and Rowse fostered and then adopted a baby boy. Later that same year, they welcomed another son into their family. The new baby, born prematurely and abandoned by his biological mother, required around-the-clock care. The next year, a baby girl with special needs joined their family. Michigan, however, permits only opposite-sex married couples or single individuals to adopt, so each child can have only one woman as his or her legal parent. If an emergency were to arise, schools and hospitals may treat the three children as if they had only one parent. And, were tragedy to befall either DeBoer or Rowse, the other would have no legal rights over the children she had not been permitted to adopt. This couple seeks relief from the continuing uncertainty their unmarried status creates in their lives.

Army Reserve Sergeant First Class Ijpe DeKoe and his partner Thomas Kostura, co-plaintiffs in the Tennessee case, fell in love. In 2011, DeKoe received orders to deploy to Afghanistan. Before leaving, he and Kostura married in New York. A week later, DeKoe began his deployment, which lasted for almost a year. When he returned, the two settled in Tennessee, where DeKoe works full-time for the Army Reserve. Their lawful marriage is stripped from them whenever they reside in Tennessee, returning and disappearing as they travel across state lines. DeKoe, who served this Nation to preserve the freedom the Constitution protects, must endure a substantial burden.

The cases now before the Court involve other petitioners as well, each with their own experiences. Their stories reveal that they seek not to denigrate marriage but rather to live their lives, or honor their spouses' memory, joined by its bond.

B

The ancient origins of marriage confirm its centrality, but it has not stood in isolation from developments in law and society. The history of marriage is one of both continuity and change. That institution—even as confined to opposite-sex relations—has evolved over time.

For example, marriage was once viewed as an arrangement by the couple's parents based on political, religious, and financial concerns; but by the time of the Nation's founding it was understood to be a voluntary contract between a man and a woman. See N. Cott, Public Vows: A History of Marriage and the Nation 9–17 (2000); S. Coontz, Marriage, A History 15–16 (2005). As the role and status of women changed, the institution further evolved. Under the centuries-old doctrine of coverture, a married man and woman were treated by the State as a single, male-dominated legal entity. See 1 W. Blackstone, Commentaries on the Laws of England 430 (1765). As women gained legal, political, and property rights, and as society began to understand that women have their own equal dignity, the law of coverture was abandoned. See Brief for Historians of Marriage et al. as *Amici Curiae* 16–19. These and other developments in the institution of marriage over the past centuries were not mere superficial changes.

Rather, they worked deep transformations in its structure, affecting aspects of marriage long viewed by many as essential. See generally N. Cott, Public Vows; S. Coontz, Marriage; H. Hartog, Man & Wife in America: A History (2000).

These new insights have strengthened, not weakened, the institution of marriage. Indeed, changed understandings of marriage are characteristic of a Nation where new dimensions of freedom become apparent to new generations, often through perspectives that begin in pleas or protests and then are considered in the political sphere and the judicial process.

This dynamic can be seen in the Nation's experiences with the rights of gays and lesbians. Until the mid-20th century, same-sex intimacy long had been condemned as immoral by the state itself in most Western nations, a belief often embodied in the criminal law. For this reason, among others, many persons did not deem homosexuals to have dignity in their own distinct identity. A truthful declaration by same-sex couples of what was in their hearts had to remain unspoken. Even when a greater awareness of the humanity and integrity of homosexual persons came in the period after World War II, the argument that gays and lesbians had a just claim to dignity was in conflict with both law and widespread social conventions. Same-sex intimacy remained a crime in many States. Gays and lesbians were prohibited from most government employment, barred from military service, excluded under immigration laws, targeted by police, and burdened in their rights to associate. See Brief for Organization of American Historians as *Amicus Curiae* 5–28.

For much of the 20th century, moreover, homosexuality was treated as an illness. When the American Psychiatric Association published the first Diagnostic and Statistical Manual of Mental Disorders in 1952, homosexuality was classified as a mental disorder, a position adhered to until 1973. See Position Statement on Homosexuality and Civil Rights, 1973, in 131 Am. J. Psychiatry 497 (1974). Only in more recent years have psychiatrists and others recognized that sexual orientation is both a normal expression of human sexuality and immutable. See Brief for American Psychological Association et al. as *Amici Curiae* 7–17.

In the late 20th century, following substantial cultural and political developments, same-sex couples began to lead more open and public lives and to establish families. This development was followed by a quite extensive discussion of the issue in both governmental and private sectors and by a shift in public attitudes toward greater tolerance. As a result, questions about the rights of gays and lesbians soon reached the courts, where the issue could be discussed in the formal discourse of the law.

This Court first gave detailed consideration to the legal status of homosexuals in *Bowers* v. *Hardwick*, 478 U. S. 186 (1986). There it upheld the constitutionality of a Georgia law deemed to criminalize certain homosexual acts. Ten years later, in *Romer* v. *Evans*, 517 U. S. 620 (1996), the Court invalidated an amendment to Colorado's Constitution that sought to foreclose any branch or political subdivision of the State from protecting persons against discrimination based on sexual orientation. Then, in 2003, the Court overruled *Bowers*, holding that laws making same-sex intimacy a crime "demea[n] the lives of homosexual persons." *Lawrence* v. *Texas*, 539 U. S. 558, 575.

Against this background, the legal question of same-sex marriage arose. In 1993, the Hawaii Supreme Court held Hawaii's law restricting marriage to opposite-sex couples constituted a classification on the basis of sex and was therefore subject to strict scrutiny under the Hawaii Constitution. *Baehr* v. *Lewin*, 74 Haw. 530, 852 P. 2d 44. Although this decision did not mandate that same-sex marriage be allowed, some States were concerned by its implications and reaffirmed in their laws that marriage is defined as a union between opposite-sex partners. So too in 1996, Congress passed the Defense of Marriage Act (DOMA), 110 Stat. 2419, defining marriage for all federal-law purposes as "only a legal union between one man and one woman as husband and wife." 1 U. S. C. §7.

The new and widespread discussion of the subject led other States to a different conclusion. In 2003, the Supreme Judicial Court of Massachusetts held the State's Constitution guaranteed same-sex couples the right to marry. See *Goodridge* v. *Department of Public Health*, 440 Mass. 309, 798 N. E. 2d 941 (2003). After that ruling, some additional States granted marriage rights to same-sex couples, either through judicial or legislative proc- esses. These decisions and statutes are cited in Appendix B, *infra*. Two Terms ago, in *United States* v. *Windsor*, 570 U. S. ___ (2013), this Court invalidated DOMA to the extent it barred the Federal Government from treating same-sex marriages as valid even when they were lawful in the State where they were licensed. DOMA, the Court held, impermissibly disparaged those same-sex couples "who wanted to affirm their commitment to one another before their children, their family, their friends, and their community." *Id.,* at ___ (slip op., at 14).

Numerous cases about same-sex marriage have reached the United States Courts of Appeals in recent years. In accordance with the judicial duty to base their decisions on principled reasons and neutral discussions, without scornful or disparaging commentary, courts have written a substantial body of law considering all sides of these issues. That case law helps to explain and formulate the underlying principles this Court now must consider. With the exception of the opinion here under review and one other, see *Citizens for Equal Protection* v. *Bruning*, 455 F. 3d 859, 864–868 (CA8 2006), the Courts of Appeals have held that excluding same-sex couples from marriage violates the Constitution. There also have been many thoughtful District Court decisions addressing same-sex marriage—and most of them, too, have concluded same-sex couples must be allowed to marry. In addition the highest courts of many States have contributed to this ongoing dialogue in decisions interpreting their own State Constitutions. These state and federal judicial opinions are cited in Appendix A, *infra*.

After years of litigation, legislation, referenda, and the discussions that attended these public acts, the States are now divided on the issue of same-sex marriage. See Office of the Atty. Gen. of Maryland, The State of Marriage Equality in America, State-by-State Supp. (2015).

III

Under the Due Process Clause of the Fourteenth Amendment, no State shall "deprive any person of life, liberty, or property, without due process of law." The fundamental liberties protected by this Clause include most of the rights enumerated in the Bill of Rights. See *Duncan* v. *Louisiana*, 391 U. S. 145, 147–149 (1968). In addition these liberties extend to certain personal choices central to individual dignity and autonomy, including intimate choices that define personal identity and beliefs. See, *e.g., Eisenstadt* v. *Baird*, 405 U. S. 438, 453 (1972); *Griswold* v. *Connecticut*, 381 U. S. 479, 484–486 (1965).

The identification and protection of fundamental rights is an enduring part of the judicial duty to interpret the Constitution. That responsibility, however, "has not been reduced to any formula." *Poe* v. *Ullman*, 367 U. S. 497, 542 (1961) (Harlan, J., dissenting). Rather, it requires courts to exercise reasoned judgment in identifying interests of the person so fundamental that the State must accord them its respect. See *ibid.* That process is guided by many of the same considerations relevant to analysis of other constitutional provisions that set forth broad principles rather than specific requirements. History and tradition guide and discipline this inquiry but do not set its outer boundaries. See *Lawrence*, *supra*, at 572. That method respects our history and learns from it without allowing the past alone to rule the present.

The nature of injustice is that we may not always see it in our own times. The generations that wrote and ratified the Bill of Rights and the Fourteenth Amendment did not presume to know the extent of freedom in all of its dimensions, and so they entrusted to future generations a charter protecting the right of all persons to enjoy liberty as we learn its meaning. When new insight reveals discord between the Constitution's central protections and a received legal stricture, a claim to liberty must be addressed.

Applying these established tenets, the Court has long held the right to marry is protected by the Constitution. In *Loving* v. *Virginia*, 388 U. S. 1, 12 (1967), which invalidated bans on interracial unions, a unanimous Court held marriage is "one of the vital personal rights essential to the orderly pursuit of happiness by free men." The Court reaffirmed that holding in *Zablocki* v. *Redhail*, 434 U. S. 374, 384 (1978), which held the right to marry was burdened by a law prohibiting fathers who were behind on child support from marrying. The Court again applied this principle in *Turner* v. *Safley*, 482 U. S. 78, 95 (1987), which held the right to marry was abridged by regulations limiting the privilege of prison inmates to marry. Over time and in other contexts, the Court has reiterated that the right to marry is fundamental under the Due Process Clause. See, *e.g., M. L. B.* v. *S. L. J.*, 519 U. S. 102, 116 (1996); *Cleveland Bd. of Ed.* v. *LaFleur*, 414 U. S. 632, 639–640 (1974); *Griswold, supra*, at 486; *Skinner* v. *Oklahoma ex rel. Williamson*, 316 U. S. 535, 541 (1942); *Meyer* v. *Nebraska*, 262 U. S. 390, 399 (1923).

It cannot be denied that this Court's cases describing the right to marry presumed a relationship involving opposite-sex partners. The Court, like many institutions, has made assumptions defined by the world and time of which it is a part. This was evident in *Baker* v. *Nelson*, 409 U. S. 810, a one-line summary decision issued in 1972, holding the exclusion of same-sex couples from marriage did not present a substantial federal question.

Still, there are other, more instructive precedents. This Court's cases have expressed constitutional principles of broader reach. In defining the right to marry these cases have identified essential attributes of that right based in history, tradition, and other constitutional liberties inherent in this intimate bond. See, *e.g., Lawrence*, 539 U. S., at 574; *Turner, supra*, at 95; *Zablocki, supra*, at 384; *Loving, supra*, at 12; *Griswold, supra*, at 486. And in assessing whether the force and rationale of its cases apply to same-sex couples, the Court must respect the basic reasons why the right to marry has been long protected. See, *e.g., Eisenstadt, supra*, at 453–454; *Poe, supra*, at 542–553 (Harlan, J., dissenting).

This analysis compels the conclusion that same-sex couples may exercise the right to marry. The four principles and traditions to be discussed demonstrate that the reasons marriage is fundamental under the Constitution apply with equal force to same-sex couples.

A first premise of the Court's relevant precedents is that the right to personal choice regarding marriage is inherent in the concept of individual autonomy. This abiding connection between marriage and liberty is why *Loving* invalidated interracial marriage bans under the Due Process Clause. See 388 U. S., at 12; see also *Zablocki, supra,* at 384 (observing *Loving* held "the right to marry is of fundamental importance for all individuals"). Like choices concerning contraception, family relationships, procreation, and childrearing, all of which are protected by the Constitution, decisions concerning marriage are among the most intimate that an individual can make. See *Lawrence, supra*, at 574. Indeed, the Court has noted it would be contradictory "to recognize a right of privacy with respect to other matters of family life and not with respect to the decision to enter the relationship that is the foundation of the family in our society." *Zablocki, supra*, at 386.

Choices about marriage shape an individual's destiny. As the Supreme Judicial Court of Massachusetts has explained, because "it fulfils yearnings for security, safe haven, and connection that express our common human- ity, civil marriage is an esteemed institution, and the decision whether and whom to marry is among life's momentous acts of self-definition." *Goodridge*, 440 Mass., at 322, 798 N. E. 2d, at 955.

The nature of marriage is that, through its enduring bond, two persons together can find other freedoms, such as expression, intimacy, and spirituality. This is true for all persons, whatever their sexual orientation. See *Windsor*, 570 U. S., at ___– ___ (slip op., at 22–23). There is dignity in the bond between two men or two women who seek to marry and in their autonomy to make such profound choices. Cf. *Loving, supra*, at 12 ("[T]he freedom to marry, or not marry, a person of another race resides with the individual and cannot be infringed by the State").

A second principle in this Court's jurisprudence is that the right to marry is fundamental because it supports a two-person union unlike any other in its importance to the committed individuals. This point was central to *Griswold* v. *Connecticut*, which held the Constitution protects the right of married couples to use contraception. 381 U. S., at 485. Suggesting that marriage is a right "older than the Bill of Rights," *Griswold* described marriage this way:

> "Marriage is a coming together for better or for worse, hopefully enduring, and intimate to the degree of being sacred. It is an association that promotes a way of life, not causes; a harmony in living, not political faiths; a bilateral loyalty, not commercial or social projects. Yet it is an association for as noble a purpose as any involved in our prior decisions. " *Id.*, at 486.

And in *Turner*, the Court again acknowledged the intimate association protected by this right, holding prisoners could not be denied the right to marry because their committed relationships satisfied the basic reasons why marriage is a fundamental right. See 482 U. S., at 95–96. The right to marry thus dignifies couples who "wish to define themselves by their commitment to each other." *Windsor, supra,* at ___ (slip op., at 14). Marriage responds to the universal fear that a lonely person might call out only to find no one there. It offers the hope of companionship and understanding and assurance that while both still live there will be someone to care for the other.

As this Court held in *Lawrence*, same-sex couples have the same right as opposite-sex couples to enjoy intimate association. *Lawrence* invalidated laws that made same-sex intimacy a criminal act. And it acknowledged that "[w]hen sexuality finds overt expression in intimate conduct with another person, the conduct can be but one element in a personal bond that is more enduring." 539

U. S., at 567. But while *Lawrence* confirmed a dimension of freedom that allows individuals to engage in intimate association without criminal liability, it does not follow that freedom stops there. Outlaw to outcast may be a step forward, but it does not achieve the full promise of liberty.

A third basis for protecting the right to marry is that it safeguards children and families and thus draws meaning from related rights of childrearing, procreation, and education. See *Pierce* v. *Society of Sisters*, 268 U. S. 510 (1925); *Meyer*, 262 U. S., at 399. The Court has recognized these connections by describing the varied rights as a unified whole: "[T]he right to 'marry, establish a home and bring up children' is a central part of the liberty protected by the Due Process Clause." *Zablocki*, 434 U. S., at 384 (quoting *Meyer*, *supra*, at 399). Under the laws of the several States, some of marriage's protections for children and families are material. But marriage also confers more profound benefits. By giving recognition and legal structure to their parents' relationship, marriage allows children "to understand the integrity and closeness of their own family and its concord with other families in their community and in their daily lives." *Windsor*, *supra,* at ___ (slip op., at 23). Marriage also affords the permanency and stability important to children's best interests. See Brief for Scholars of the Constitutional Rights of Children as *Amici Curiae* 22–27.

As all parties agree, many same-sex couples provide loving and nurturing homes to their children, whether biological or adopted. And hundreds of thousands of children are presently being raised by such couples. See Brief for Gary J. Gates as *Amicus Curiae* 4. Most States have allowed gays and lesbians to adopt, either as individuals or as couples, and many adopted and foster children have same-sex parents, see *id.,* at 5. This provides powerful confirmation from the law itself that gays and lesbians can create loving, supportive families.

Excluding same-sex couples from marriage thus conflicts with a central premise of the right to marry. Without the recognition, stability, and predictability marriage offers, their children suffer the stigma of knowing their families are somehow lesser. They also suffer the significant material costs of being raised by unmarried parents, relegated through no fault of their own to a more difficult and uncertain family life. The marriage laws at issue here thus harm and humiliate the children of same-sex couples. See *Windsor*, *supra,* at ___ (slip op., at 23).

That is not to say the right to marry is less meaningful for those who do not or cannot have children. An ability, desire, or promise to procreate is not and has not been a prerequisite for a valid marriage in any State. In light of precedent protecting the right of a married couple not to procreate, it cannot be said the Court or the States have conditioned the right to marry on the capacity or commitment to procreate. The constitutional marriage right has many aspects, of which childbearing is only one.

Fourth and finally, this Court's cases and the Nation's traditions make clear that marriage is a keystone of our social order. Alexis de Tocqueville recognized this truth on his travels through the United States almost two centuries ago:

> "There is certainly no country in the world where the tie of marriage is so much respected as in America . . . [W]hen the American retires from the turmoil of public life to the bosom of his family, he finds in it the image of order and of peace . . . . [H]e afterwards carries [that image] with him into public affairs." 1 Democ- racy in America 309 (H. Reeve transl., rev. ed. 1990).

In *Maynard* v. *Hill*, 125 U. S. 190, 211 (1888), the Court echoed de Tocqueville, explaining that marriage is "the foundation of the family and of society, without which there would be neither civilization nor progress." Marriage, the *Maynard* Court said, has long been "'a great public institution, giving character to our whole civil polity.'" *Id.,* at 213. This idea has been reiterated even as the institution has evolved in substantial ways over time, superseding rules related to parental consent, gender, and race once thought by many to be essential. See generally N. Cott, Public Vows. Marriage remains a building block of our national community.

For that reason, just as a couple vows to support each other, so does society pledge to support the couple, offering symbolic recognition and material benefits to protect and nourish the union. Indeed, while the States are in general free to vary the benefits they confer on all married couples, they have throughout our history made marriage the basis for an expanding list of governmental rights, benefits, and responsibilities. These aspects of marital status include: taxation; inheritance and property rights; rules of intestate succession; spousal privilege in the law of evidence; hospital access; medical decisionmaking authority; adoption rights; the rights and benefits of survivors; birth and death certificates; professional ethics rules; campaign finance restrictions; workers' compensation benefits; health insurance; and child custody, support, and visitation rules. See Brief for United States as *Amicus Curiae* 6–9; Brief for American Bar Association as *Amicus Curiae* 8–29. Valid marriage under state law is also a significant status for over a thousand provisions of federal law. See *Windsor*, 570 U. S., at ___ – ___ (slip op., at 15–16). The States have contributed to the fundamental character of the marriage right by placing that institution at the center of so many facets of the legal and social order.

There is no difference between same- and opposite-sex couples with respect to this principle. Yet by virtue of their exclusion from that institution, same-sex couples are denied the constellation of benefits that the States have linked to marriage. This harm results in more than just material burdens. Same-sex couples are consigned to an instability many opposite-sex couples would deem intolerable in their own lives. As the State itself makes marriage all the more precious by the significance it attaches to it, exclusion from that status has the effect of teaching that gays and lesbians are unequal in important respects. It demeans gays and lesbians for the State to lock them out of a central institution of the Nation's society. Same-sex couples, too, may aspire to the transcendent purposes of marriage and seek fulfillment in its highest meaning.

The limitation of marriage to opposite-sex couples may long have seemed natural and just, but its inconsistency with the central meaning of the fundamental right to marry is now manifest. With that knowledge must come the recognition that laws excluding same-sex couples from the marriage right impose stigma and injury of the kind prohibited by our basic charter.

Objecting that this does not reflect an appropriate framing of the issue, the respondents refer to *Washington* v. *Glucksberg*, 521 U. S. 702, 721 (1997), which called for a "'careful description'" of fundamental rights. They assert the petitioners do not seek to exercise the right to marry but rather a new and nonexistent "right to same-sex marriage." Brief for Respondent in No. 14–556, p. 8. *Glucksberg* did insist that liberty under the Due Process Clause must be defined in a most circumscribed manner, with central reference to specific historical practices. Yet while that approach may have been appropriate for the asserted right there involved (physician-assisted suicide), it is inconsistent with the approach this Court has used in discussing other fundamental rights, including marriage and intimacy. *Loving* did not ask about a "right to interracial marriage"; *Turner* did not ask about a "right of inmates to marry"; and *Zablocki* did not ask about a "right of fathers with unpaid child support duties to marry." Rather, each case inquired about the right to marry in its comprehensive sense, asking if there was a sufficient justification for excluding the relevant class from the right. See also *Glucksberg*, 521 U. S., at 752–773 (Souter, J., concurring in judgment); *id.,* at 789–792 (BREYER, J., concurring in judgments).

That principle applies here. If rights were defined by who exercised them in the past, then received practices could serve as their own continued justification and new groups could not invoke rights once denied. This Court has rejected that approach, both with respect to the right to marry and the rights of gays and lesbians. See *Loving* 388 U. S., at 12; *Lawrence*, 539 U. S., at 566–567.

The right to marry is fundamental as a matter of history and tradition, but rights come not from ancient sources alone. They rise, too, from a better informed understanding of how constitutional imperatives define a liberty that remains urgent in our own era. Many who deem same-sex marriage to be wrong reach that conclusion based on decent and honorable religious or philosophical premises, and neither they nor their beliefs are disparaged here. But when that sincere, personal opposition becomes en- acted law and public policy, the necessary consequence is to put the imprimatur of the State itself on an exclusion that soon demeans or stigmatizes those whose own liberty is then denied. Under the Constitution, same-sex couples seek in marriage the same legal treatment as opposite-sex couples, and it would disparage their choices and diminish their personhood to deny them this right.

The right of same-sex couples to marry that is part of the liberty promised by the Fourteenth Amendment is derived, too, from that Amendment's guarantee of the equal protection of the laws. The Due Process Clause and the Equal Protection Clause are connected in a profound way, though they set forth independent principles. Rights implicit in liberty and rights secured by equal protection may rest on different precepts and are not always coextensive, yet in some instances each may be instructive as to the meaning and reach of the other. In any particular case one Clause may be thought to capture the essence of the right in a more accurate and comprehensive way, even as the two Clauses may converge in the identification and definition of the right. See *M. L. B.*, 519 U. S., at 120– 121; *id.*, at 128–129 (KENNEDY, J., concurring in judgment); *Bearden* v. *Georgia*, 461 U. S. 660, 665 (1983). This interrelation of the two principles furthers our understanding of what freedom is and must become.

The Court's cases touching upon the right to marry reflect this dynamic. In *Loving* the Court invalidated a prohibition on interracial marriage under both the Equal Protection Clause and the Due Process Clause. The Court first declared the prohibition invalid because of its unequal treatment of interracial couples. It stated: "There can be no doubt that restricting the freedom to marry solely because of racial classifications violates the central meaning of the Equal Protection Clause." 388 U. S., at 12. With this link to equal protection the Court proceeded to hold the prohibition offended central precepts of liberty: "To deny this fundamental freedom on so unsupportable a basis as the racial classifications embodied in these statutes, classifications so directly subversive of the principle of equality at the heart of the Fourteenth Amendment, is surely to deprive all the State's citizens of liberty without due process of law." *Ibid.* The reasons why marriage is a fundamental right became more clear and compelling from a full awareness and understanding of the hurt that resulted from laws barring interracial unions.

The synergy between the two protections is illustrated further in *Zablocki*. There the Court invoked the Equal Protection Clause as its basis for invalidating the challenged law, which, as already noted, barred fathers who were behind on child-support payments from marrying without judicial approval. The equal protection analysis depended in central part on the Court's holding that the law burdened a right "of fundamental importance." 434 U. S., at 383. It was the essential nature of the marriage right, discussed at length in *Zablocki*, see *id.,* at 383–387, that made apparent the law's incompatibility with requirements of equality. Each concept—liberty and equal protection—leads to a stronger understanding of the other.

Indeed, in interpreting the Equal Protection Clause, the Court has recognized that new insights and societal understandings can reveal unjustified inequality within our most fundamental institutions that once passed unnoticed and unchallenged. To take but one period, this occurred with respect to marriage in the 1970's and 1980's. Notwithstanding the gradual erosion of the doctrine of coverture, see *supra*, at 6, invidious sex-based classifications in marriage remained common through the mid-20th century. See App. to Brief for Appellant in *Reed* v. *Reed*, O. T. 1971, No. 70–4, pp. 69–88 (an extensive reference to laws extant as of 1971 treating women as unequal to men in marriage). These classifications denied the equal dignity of men and women. One State's law, for example, pro- vided in 1971 that "the husband is the head of the family and the wife is subject to him; her legal civil existence is merged in the husband, except so far as the law recognizes her separately, either for her own protection, or for her benefit." Ga. Code Ann. §53–501 (1935). Responding to a new awareness, the Court invoked equal protection principles to invalidate laws imposing sex-based inequality on marriage. See, *e.g., Kirchberg* v. *Feenstra*, 450 U. S. 455 (1981); *Wengler* v. *Druggists Mut. Ins. Co.*, 446 U. S. 142 (1980); *Califano* v. *Westcott*, 443 U. S. 76 (1979); *Orr* v. *Orr*, 440 U. S. 268 (1979); *Califano* v. *Goldfarb*, 430 U. S. 199 (1977) (plurality opinion); *Weinberger* v. *Wiesenfeld*, 420 U. S. 636 (1975); *Frontiero* v. *Richardson*, 411 U. S. 677 (1973). Like *Loving* and *Zablocki*, these precedents show the Equal Protection Clause can help to identify and correct inequalities in the institution of marriage, vindicating precepts of liberty and equality under the Constitution.

Other cases confirm this relation between liberty and equality. In *M. L. B.* v. *S. L. J.*, the Court invalidated under due process and equal protection principles a statute requiring indigent mothers to pay a fee in order to appeal the termination of their parental rights. See 519 U. S., at 119–124. In *Eisenstadt* v. *Baird*, the Court invoked both principles to invalidate a prohibition on the distribution of contraceptives to unmarried persons but not married persons. See 405 U. S., at 446–454. And in *Skinner* v. *Oklahoma ex rel. Williamson*, the Court invalidated under both principles a law that allowed sterilization of habitual criminals. See 316 U. S., at 538–543.

In *Lawrence* the Court acknowledged the interlocking nature of these constitutional safeguards in the context of the legal treatment of gays and lesbians. See 539 U. S., at 575. Although *Lawrence* elaborated its holding under the Due Process Clause, it acknowledged, and sought to rem- edy, the continuing inequality that resulted from laws making intimacy in the lives of gays and lesbians a crime against the State. See *ibid. Lawrence* therefore drew upon principles of liberty and equality to define and protect the rights of gays and lesbians, holding the State "cannot demean their existence or control their destiny by making their private sexual conduct a crime." *Id.*, at 578.

This dynamic also applies to same-sex marriage. It is now clear that the challenged laws burden the liberty of same-sex couples, and it must be further acknowledged that they abridge central precepts of equality. Here the marriage laws enforced by the respondents are in essence unequal: same-sex couples are denied all the benefits afforded to opposite-sex couples and are barred from exercising a fundamental right. Especially against a long history of disapproval of their relationships, this denial to same-sex couples of the right to marry works a grave and continuing harm. The imposition of this disability on gays and lesbians serves to disrespect and subordinate them. And the Equal Protection Clause, like the Due Process Clause, prohibits this unjustified infringement of the fundamental right to marry. See, *e.g., Zablocki*, *supra*, at 383–388; *Skinner*, 316 U. S., at 541.

These considerations lead to the conclusion that the right to marry is a fundamental right inherent in the liberty of the person, and under the Due Process and Equal Protection Clauses of the Fourteenth Amendment couples of the same-sex may not be deprived of that right and that liberty. The Court now holds that same-sex couples may exercise the fundamental right to marry. No longer may this liberty be denied to them. *Baker* v. *Nelson* must be and now is overruled, and the State laws challenged by Petitioners in these cases are now held invalid to the extent they exclude same-sex couples from civil marriage on the same terms and conditions as opposite-sex couples.

IV

There may be an initial inclination in these cases to proceed with caution—to await further legislation, litigation, and debate. The respondents warn there has been insufficient democratic discourse before deciding an issue so basic as the definition of marriage. In its ruling on the cases now before this Court, the majority opinion for the Court of Appeals made a cogent argument that it would be appropriate for the respondents' States to await further public discussion and political measures before licensing same-sex marriages. See *DeBoer*, 772 F. 3d, at 409.

Yet there has been far more deliberation than this argument acknowledges. There have been referenda, legislative debates, and grassroots campaigns, as well as countless studies, papers, books, and other popular and scholarly writings. There has been extensive litigation in state and federal courts. See Appendix A, *infra*. Judicial opinions addressing the issue have been informed by the contentions of parties and counsel, which, in turn, reflect the more general, societal discussion of same-sex marriage and its meaning that has occurred over the past decades. As more than 100 *amici* make clear in their filings, many of the central institutions in American life—state and local governments, the military, large and small businesses, labor unions, religious organizations, law enforcement, civic groups, professional organizations, and universities— have devoted substantial attention to the question. This has led to an enhanced understanding of the issue—an understanding reflected in the arguments now presented for resolution as a matter of constitutional law.

Of course, the Constitution contemplates that democracy is the appropriate process for change, so long as that process does not abridge fundamental rights. Last Term, a plurality of this Court reaffirmed the importance of the democratic principle in *Schuette* v. *BAMN*, 572 U. S. ___ (2014), noting the "right of citizens to debate so they can learn and decide and then, through the political process, act in concert to try to shape the course of their own times." *Id.*, at ___ – ___ (slip op., at 15–16). Indeed, it is most often through democracy that liberty is preserved and protected in our lives. But as *Schuette* also said, "[t]he freedom secured by the Constitution consists, in one of its essential dimensions, of the right of the individual not to be injured by the unlawful exercise of governmental power." *Id.*, at ___ (slip op., at 15). Thus, when the rights of persons are violated, "the Constitution requires redress by the courts," notwithstanding the more general value of democratic decisionmaking. *Id.,* at ___ (slip op., at 17). This holds true even when protecting individual rights affects issues of the utmost importance and sensitivity.

The dynamic of our constitutional system is that individuals need not await legislative action before asserting a fundamental right. The Nation's courts are open to injured individuals who come to them to vindicate their own direct, personal stake in our basic charter. An individual can invoke a right to constitutional protection when he or she is harmed, even if the broader public disagrees and even if the legislature refuses to act. The idea of the Constitution "was to withdraw certain subjects from the vicissitudes of political controversy, to place them beyond the reach of majorities and officials and to establish them as legal principles to be applied by the courts." *West Virginia Bd. of Ed.* v. *Barnette*, 319 U. S. 624, 638 (1943). This is why "fundamental rights may not be submitted to a vote; they depend on the outcome of no elections." *Ibid.*

It is of no moment whether advocates of same-sex marriage now enjoy or lack momentum in the democratic process. The issue before the Court here is the legal question whether the Constitution protects the right of same-sex couples to marry.

This is not the first time the Court has been asked to adopt a cautious approach to recognizing and protecting fundamental rights. In *Bowers*, a bare majority upheld a law criminalizing same-sex intimacy. See 478 U. S., at 186, 190–195. That approach might have been viewed as a cautious endorsement of the democratic process, which had only just begun to consider the rights of gays and lesbians. Yet, in effect, *Bowers* upheld state action that denied gays and lesbians a fundamental right and caused them pain and humiliation. As evidenced by the dissents in that case, the facts and principles necessary to a correct holding were known to the *Bowers* Court. See *id.*, at 199 (Blackmun, J., joined by Brennan, Marshall, and Stevens, JJ., dissenting); *id.,* at 214 (Stevens, J., joined by Brennan and Marshall, JJ., dissenting). That is why *Lawrence* held *Bowers* was "not correct when it was decided." 539 U. S., at 578. Although *Bowers* was eventually repudiated in *Lawrence*, men and women were harmed in the interim, and the substantial effects of these injuries no doubt lingered long after *Bowers* was overruled. Dignitary wounds cannot always be healed with the stroke of a pen.

A ruling against same-sex couples would have the same effect—and, like *Bowers*, would be unjustified under the Fourteenth Amendment. The petitioners' stories make clear the urgency of the issue they present to the Court. James Obergefell now asks whether Ohio can erase his marriage to John Arthur for all time. April DeBoer and Jayne Rowse now ask whether Michigan may continue to deny them the certainty and stability all mothers desire to protect their children, and for them and their children the childhood years will pass all too soon. Ijpe DeKoe and Thomas Kostura now ask whether Tennessee can deny to one who has served this Nation the basic dignity of recognizing his New York marriage. Properly presented with the petitioners' cases, the Court has a duty to address these claims and answer these questions.

Indeed, faced with a disagreement among the Courts of Appeals—a disagreement that caused impermissible geographic variation in the meaning of federal law—the Court granted review to determine whether same-sex couples may exercise the right to marry. Were the Court to uphold the challenged laws as constitutional, it would teach the Nation that these laws are in accord with our society's most basic compact. Were the Court to stay its hand to allow slower, case-by-case determination of the required availability of specific public benefits to same-sex couples, it still would deny gays and lesbians many rights and responsibilities intertwined with marriage.

The respondents also argue allowing same-sex couples to wed will harm marriage as an institution by leading to fewer opposite-sex marriages. This may occur, the respondents contend, because licensing same-sex marriage severs the connection between natural procreation and marriage. That argument, however, rests on a counterintuitive view of opposite-sex couple's decisionmaking processes regarding marriage and parenthood. Decisions about whether to marry and raise children are based on many personal, romantic, and practical considerations; and it is unrealistic to conclude that an opposite-sex couple would choose not to marry simply because same-sex couples may do so. See *Kitchen* v. *Herbert*, 755 F. 3d 1193, 1223 (CA10 2014) ("[I]t is wholly illogical to believe that state recognition of the love and commitment between same-sex couples will alter the most intimate and personal decisions of opposite-sex couples"). The respondents have not shown a foundation for the conclusion that allowing same-sex marriage will cause the harmful outcomes they describe. Indeed, with respect to this asserted basis for excluding same-sex couples from the right to marry, it is appropriate to observe these cases involve only the rights of two consenting adults whose marriages would pose no risk of harm to themselves or third parties.

Finally, it must be emphasized that religions, and those who adhere to religious doctrines, may continue to advocate with utmost, sincere conviction that, by divine precepts, same-sex marriage should not be condoned. The First Amendment ensures that religious organizations and persons are given proper protection as they seek to teach the principles that are so fulfilling and so central to their lives and faiths, and to their own deep aspirations to continue the family structure they have long revered. The same is true of those who oppose same-sex marriage for other reasons. In turn, those who believe allowing same-sex marriage is proper or indeed essential, whether as a matter of religious conviction or secular belief, may engage those who disagree with their view in an open and searching debate. The Constitution, however, does not permit the State to bar same-sex couples from marriage on the same terms as accorded to couples of the opposite sex.

V

These cases also present the question whether the Constitution requires States to recognize same-sex marriages validly performed out of State. As made clear by the case of Obergefell and Arthur, and by that of DeKoe and Kos- tura, the recognition bans inflict substantial and continuing harm on same-sex couples.

Being married in one State but having that valid marriage denied in another is one of "the most perplexing and distressing complication[s]" in the law of domestic relations. *Williams* v. *North Carolina*, 317 U. S. 287, 299 (1942) (internal quotation marks omitted). Leaving the current state of affairs in place would maintain and promote instability and uncertainty. For some couples, even an ordinary drive into a neighboring State to visit family or friends risks causing severe hardship in the event of a spouse's hospitalization while across state lines. In light of the fact that many States already allow same-sex marriage—and hundreds of thousands of these marriages already have occurred—the disruption caused by the recognition bans is significant and ever-growing.

As counsel for the respondents acknowledged at argument, if States are required by the Constitution to issue marriage licenses to same-sex couples, the justifications for refusing to recognize those marriages performed else-where are undermined. See Tr. of Oral Arg. on Question 2, p. 44. The Court, in this decision, holds same-sex couples may exercise the fundamental right to marry in all States. It follows that the Court also must hold—and it now does hold—that there is no lawful basis for a State to refuse to recognize a lawful same-sex marriage performed in another State on the ground of its same-sex character.

* * *

No union is more profound than marriage, for it embodies the highest ideals of love, fidelity, devotion, sacrifice, and family. In forming a marital union, two people become something greater than once they were. As some of the petitioners in these cases demonstrate, marriage embodies a love that may endure even past death. It would misunderstand these men and women to say they disrespect the idea of marriage. Their plea is that they do respect it, respect it so deeply that they seek to find its fulfillment for themselves. Their hope is not to be condemned to live in loneliness, excluded from one of civilization's oldest institutions. They ask for equal dignity in the eyes of the law. The Constitution grants them that right.

The judgment of the Court of Appeals for the Sixth Circuit is reversed.

It is so ordered.

APPENDIX A TO OPINION OF THE COURT

APPENDICES

A

State and Federal Judicial Decisions
Addressing Same-Sex Marriage

United States Courts of Appeals Decisions

Adams v. *Howerton*, 673 F. 2d 1036 (CA9 1982)
Smelt v. *County of Orange*, 447 F. 3d 673 (CA9 2006)
Citizens for Equal Protection v. *Bruning*, 455 F. 3d 859 (CA8 2006)
Windsor v. *United States*, 699 F. 3d 169 (CA2 2012)
Massachusetts v. *Department of Health and Human Services*, 682 F. 3d 1 (CA1 2012)
Perry v. *Brown*, 671 F. 3d 1052 (CA9 2012)

Latta v. *Otter*, 771 F. 3d 456 (CA9 2014)
Baskin v. *Bogan*, 766 F. 3d 648 (CA7 2014)
Bishop v. *Smith*, 760 F. 3d 1070 (CA10 2014)
Bostic v. *Schaefer*, 760 F. 3d 352 (CA4 2014)
Kitchen v. *Herbert*, 755 F. 3d 1193 (CA10 2014)
DeBoer v. *Snyder*, 772 F. 3d 388 (CA6 2014)
Latta v. *Otter*, 779 F. 3d 902 (CA9 2015) (O'Scannlain, J., dissenting from the denial of rehearing en banc)

United States District Court Decisions

Adams v. *Howerton*, 486 F. Supp. 1119 (CD Cal. 1980) *Citizens for Equal Protection, Inc.* v. *Bruning*, 290 F. Supp. 2d 1004 (Neb. 2003)

Citizens for Equal Protection v. *Bruning*, 368 F. Supp. 2d 980 (Neb. 2005)

Wilson v. *Ake*, 354 F. Supp. 2d 1298 (MD Fla. 2005) *Smelt* v. *County of Orange*, 374 F. Supp. 2d 861 (CD Cal. 2005)

Bishop v. *Oklahoma ex rel. Edmondson*, 447 F. Supp. 2d 1239 (ND Okla. 2006)

Massachusetts v. *Department of Health and Human Services*, 698 F. Supp. 2d 234 (Mass. 2010)

Gill v. *Office of Personnel Management*, 699 F. Supp. 2d 374 (Mass. 2010)

Perry v. *Schwarzenegger*, 704 F. Supp. 2d 921 (ND Cal. 2010)

Dragovich v. *Department of Treasury*, 764 F. Supp. 2d 1178 (ND Cal. 2011)

Golinski v. *Office of Personnel Management*, 824 F. Supp. 2d 968 (ND Cal. 2012)

Dragovich v. *Department of Treasury*, 872 F. Supp. 2d 944 (ND Cal. 2012)

Windsor v. *United States*, 833 F. Supp. 2d 394 (SDNY 2012)

Pedersen v. *Office of Personnel Management*, 881 F. Supp. 2d 294 (Conn. 2012)

Jackson v. *Abercrombie*, 884 F. Supp. 2d 1065 (Haw. 2012)

Sevcik v. *Sandoval*, 911 F. Supp. 2d 996 (Nev. 2012) *Merritt* v. *Attorney General*, 2013 WL 6044329 (MD La., Nov. 14, 2013)

Gray v. *Orr*, 4 F. Supp. 3d 984 (ND Ill. 2013)

Lee v. *Orr*, 2013 WL 6490577 (ND Ill., Dec. 10, 2013) *Kitchen* v. *Herbert*, 961 F. Supp. 2d 1181 (Utah 2013) *Obergefell* v. *Wymyslo*, 962 F. Supp. 2d 968 (SD Ohio 2013)

Bishop v. *United States ex rel. Holder*, 962 F. Supp. 2d 1252 (ND Okla. 2014)

Bourke v. *Beshear*, 996 F. Supp. 2d 542 (WD Ky. 2014) *Lee* v. *Orr*, 2014 WL 683680 (ND Ill., Feb. 21, 2014) *Bostic* v. *Rainey*, 970 F. Supp. 2d 456 (ED Va. 2014) *De Leon* v. *Perry*, 975 F. Supp. 2d 632 (WD Tex. 2014) *Tanco* v. *Haslam*, 7 F. Supp. 3d 759 (MD Tenn. 2014) *DeBoer* v. *Snyder*, 973 F. Supp. 2d 757 (ED Mich. 2014) *Henry* v. *Himes*, 14 F. Supp. 3d 1036 (SD Ohio 2014) *Latta* v. *Otter*, 19 F. Supp. 3d 1054 (Idaho 2014)

Geiger v. *Kitzhaber*, 994 F. Supp. 2d 1128 (Ore. 2014) *Evans* v. *Utah*, 21 F. Supp. 3d 1192 (Utah 2014) *Whitewood* v. *Wolf*, 992 F. Supp. 2d 410 (MD Pa. 2014) *Wolf* v. *Walker*, 986 F. Supp. 2d 982 (WD Wis. 2014) *Baskin* v. *Bogan*, 12 F. Supp. 3d 1144 (SD Ind. 2014) *Love* v. *Beshear*, 989 F. Supp. 2d 536 (WD Ky. 2014) *Burns* v. *Hickenlooper*, 2014 WL 3634834 (Colo., July 23, 2014)

Bowling v. *Pence*, 39 F. Supp. 3d 1025 (SD Ind. 2014) *Brenner* v. *Scott*, 999 F. Supp. 2d 1278 (ND Fla. 2014) *Robicheaux* v. *Caldwell*, 2 F. Supp. 3d 910 (ED La. 2014) *General Synod of the United Church of Christ* v. *Resinger*, 12 F. Supp. 3d 790 (WDNC 2014)

Hamby v. *Parnell*, 56 F. Supp. 3d 1056 (Alaska 2014) *Fisher-Borne* v. *Smith*, 14 F. Supp. 3d 695 (MDNC 2014) *Majors* v. *Horne*, 14 F. Supp. 3d 1313 (Ariz. 2014) *Connolly* v. *Jeanes*, ___ F. Supp. 3d ___, 2014 WL 5320642 (Ariz., Oct. 17, 2014)

Guzzo v. *Mead*, 2014 WL 5317797 (Wyo., Oct. 17, 2014) *Conde-Vidal* v. *Garcia-Padilla*, 54 F. Supp. 3d 157 (PR 2014)

Marie v. *Moser*, ___ F. Supp. 3d ___, 2014 WL 5598128 (Kan., Nov. 4, 2014)

Lawson v. *Kelly*, 58 F. Supp. 3d 923 (WD Mo. 2014) *McGee* v. *Cole*, ___ F. Supp. 3d ___, 2014 WL 5802665 (SD W. Va., Nov. 7, 2014)

Condon v. *Haley*, 21 F. Supp. 3d 572 (S.C. 2014)

Bradacs v. *Haley*, 58 F. Supp. 3d 514 (S.C. 2014) *Rolando* v. *Fox*, 23 F. Supp. 3d 1227 (Mont. 2014) *Jernigan* v. *Crane*, ___ F. Supp. 3d ___, 2014 WL 6685391 (ED Ark., Nov. 25, 2014)

Campaign for Southern Equality v. *Bryant*, ___ F. Supp. 3d ___, 2014 WL 6680570 (SD Miss., Nov. 25, 2014)

Inniss v. *Aderhold*, ___ F. Supp. 3d ___, 2015 WL 300593 (ND Ga., Jan. 8, 2015)

Rosenbrahn v. *Daugaard*, 61 F. Supp. 3d 862 (S. D., 2015)

Caspar v. *Snyder*, ___ F. Supp. 3d ___, 2015 WL 224741 (ED Mich., Jan. 15, 2015)

Searcey v. *Strange*, 2015 U. S. Dist. LEXIS 7776 (SD Ala., Jan. 23, 2015)

Strawser v. *Strange*, 44 F. Supp. 3d 1206 (SD Ala. 2015) *Waters* v. *Ricketts*, 48 F. Supp. 3d 1271 (Neb. 2015)

State Highest Court Decisions

Baker v. *Nelson*, 291 Minn. 310, 191 N. W. 2d 185 (1971) *Jones* v. *Hallahan*, 501 S. W. 2d 588 (Ky. 1973)

Baehr v. *Lewin*, 74 Haw. 530, 852 P. 2d 44 (1993) *Dean* v. *District of Columbia*, 653 A. 2d 307 (D. C. 1995) *Baker* v. *State*, 170 Vt. 194, 744 A. 2d 864 (1999) *Brause* v. *State*, 21 P. 3d 357 (Alaska 2001) (ripeness) *Goodridge* v. *Department of Public Health*, 440 Mass. 309, 798 N. E. 2d 941 (2003)

In re Opinions of the Justices to the Senate, 440 Mass. 1201, 802 N. E. 2d 565 (2004)

Li v. *State*, 338 Or. 376, 110 P. 3d 91 (2005) *Cote-Whitacre* v. *Department of Public Health*,446 Mass. 350, 844 N. E. 2d 623 (2006)

Lewis v. *Harris*, 188 N. J. 415, 908 A. 2d 196 (2006) *Andersen* v. *King County*, 158 Wash. 2d 1, 138 P. 3d 963 (2006)

Hernandez v. *Robles*, 7 N. Y. 3d 338, 855 N. E. 2d 1 (2006)

Conaway v. *Deane*, 401 Md. 219, 932 A. 2d 571 (2007)

In re Marriage Cases, 43 Cal. 4th 757, 183 P. 3d 384 (2008)

Kerrigan v. *Commissioner of Public Health*, 289 Conn. 135, 957 A. 2d 407 (2008)

Strauss v. *Horton*, 46 Cal. 4th 364, 207 P. 3d 48 (2009)

Varnum v. *Brien*, 763 N. W. 2d 862 (Iowa 2009)

Griego v. *Oliver*, 2014–NMSC–003, ___ N. M. ___, 316 P. 3d 865 (2013)

Garden State Equality v. *Dow*, 216 N. J. 314, 79 A. 3d 1036 (2013)

Ex parte State ex rel. Alabama Policy Institute, ___ So. 3d ___, 2015 WL 892752 (Ala., Mar. 3, 2015)

APPENDIX B TO OPINION OF THE COURT

B

State Legislation and Judicial Decisions
Legalizing Same-Sex Marriage

Legislation

Del. Code Ann., Tit. 13, §129 (Cum. Supp. 2014)
D. C. Act No. 18–248, 57 D. C. Reg. 27 (2010)
Haw. Rev. Stat. §572 –1 (2006) and 2013 Cum. Supp.)
Ill. Pub. Act No. 98–597
Me. Rev. Stat. Ann., Tit. 19, §650–A (Cum. Supp. 2014)
2012 Md. Laws p. 9
2013 Minn Laws p. 404
2009 N. H. Laws p. 60
2011 N. Y Laws p. 749
2013 R. I. Laws p. 7
2009 Vt. Acts & Resolves p. 33
2012 Wash. Sess. Laws p. 199

Judicial Decisions

Goodridge v. *Department of Public Health*, 440 Mass. 309, 798 N. E. 2d 941 (2003)

Kerrigan v. *Commissioner of Public Health*, 289 Conn. 135, 957 A. 2d 407 (2008)

Varnum v. *Brien*, 763 N. W. 2d 862 (Iowa 2009)

Griego v. *Oliver*, 2014–NMSC–003, ___ N. M. ___, 316 P. 3d 865 (2013)

Garden State Equality v. *Dow*, 216 N. J. 314, 79 A. 3d 1036 (2013)

ROBERTS, C. J., DISSENTING

SUPREME COURT OF THE UNITED STATES

Nos. 14–556, 14-562, 14-571 and 14–574

JAMES OBERGEFELL, ET AL., PETITIONERS

14–556 *v.*

RICHARD HODGES, DIRECTOR, OHIO DEPARTMENT OF HEALTH, ET AL.;

VALERIA TANCO, ET AL., PETITIONERS

14–562 *v.*

BILL HASLAM, GOVERNOR OF TENNESSEE, ET AL.;

APRIL DEBOER, ET AL., PETITIONERS

14–571 *v.*

RICK SNYDER, GOVERNOR OF MICHIGAN, ET AL.; AND

GREGORY BOURKE, ET AL., PETITIONERS

14–574 *v.*

STEVE BESHEAR, GOVERNOR OF KENTUCKY

ON WRITS OF CERTIORARI TO THE UNITED STATES COURT OF APPEALS FOR THE SIXTH CIRCUIT

[June 26, 2015]

CHIEF JUSTICE ROBERTS, with whom JUSTICE SCALIA and JUSTICE THOMAS join, dissenting.

Petitioners make strong arguments rooted in social policy and considerations of fairness. They contend that same-sex couples should be allowed to affirm their love and commitment through marriage, just like opposite-sex couples. That position has undeniable appeal; over the past six years, voters and legislators in eleven States and the District of Columbia have revised their laws to allow marriage between two people of the same sex.

But this Court is not a legislature. Whether same-sex marriage is a good idea should be of no concern to us. Under the Constitution, judges have power to say what the law is, not what it should be. The people who ratified the Constitution authorized courts to exercise "neither force nor will but merely judgment." The Federalist No. 78, p. 465 (C. Rossiter ed. 1961) (A. Hamilton) (capitalization altered).

Although the policy arguments for extending marriage to same-sex couples may be compelling, the legal arguments for requiring such an extension are not. The fundamental right to marry does not include a right to make a State change its definition of marriage. And a State's decision to maintain the meaning of marriage that has persisted in every culture throughout human history can hardly be called irrational. In short, our Constitution does not enact any one theory of marriage. The people of a State are free to expand marriage to include same-sex couples, or to retain the historic definition.

Today, however, the Court takes the extraordinary step of ordering every State to license and recognize same-sex marriage. Many people will rejoice at this decision, and I begrudge none their celebration. But for those who believe in a government of laws, not of men, the majority's approach is deeply disheartening. Supporters of same-sex marriage have achieved considerable success persuading their fellow citizens—through the democratic process—to adopt their view. That ends today. Five lawyers have closed the debate and enacted their own vision of marriage as a matter of constitutional law. Stealing this issue from the people will for many cast a cloud over same-sex marriage, making a dramatic social change that much more difficult to accept.

The majority's decision is an act of will, not legal judgment. The right it announces has no basis in the Constitution or this Court's precedent. The majority expressly disclaims judicial "caution" and omits even a pretense of humility, openly relying on its desire to remake society according to its own "new insight" into the "nature of injustice." *Antc*, at 11, 23. As a rcsult, the Court invalidates the marriage laws of more than half the States and orders the transformation of a social institution that has formed the basis of human society for millennia, for the Kalahari Bushmen and the Han Chinese, the Carthagin- ians and the Aztecs. Just who do we think we are?

It can be tempting for judges to confuse our own preferences with the requirements of the law. But as this Court has been reminded throughout our history, the Constitution "is made for people of fundamentally differing views." *Lochner* v. *New York*, 198 U. S. 45, 76 (1905) (Holmes, J., dissenting). Accordingly, "courts are not concerned with the wisdom or policy of legislation." *Id.*, at 69 (Harlan, J., dissenting). The majority today neglects that restrained conception of the judicial role. It seizes for itself a question the Constitution leaves to the people, at a time when the people are engaged in a vibrant debate on that question. And it answers that question based not on neutral principles of constitutional law, but on its own "understanding of what freedom is and must become." *Ante*, at 19. I have no choice but to dissent.

Understand well what this dissent is about: It is not about whether, in my judgment, the institution of marriage should be changed to include same-sex couples. It is instead about whether, in our democratic republic, that decision should rest with the people acting through their elected representatives, or with five lawyers who happen to hold commissions authorizing them to resolve legal disputes according to law. The Constitution leaves no doubt about the answer.

I

Petitioners and their *amici* base their arguments on the "right to marry" and the imperative of "marriage equality." There is no serious dispute that, under our precedents, the Constitution protects a right to marry and requires States to apply their marriage laws equally. The real question in these cases is what constitutes "marriage," or—more precisely—*who decides* what constitutes "marriage"?

The majority largely ignores these questions, relegating ages of human experience with marriage to a paragraph or two. Even if history and precedent are not "the end" of these cases, *ante*, at 4, I would not "sweep away what has so long been settled" without showing greater respect for all that preceded us. *Town of Greece* v. *Galloway*, 572 U. S. ___, ___ (2014) (slip op., at 8).

A

As the majority acknowledges, marriage "has existed for millennia and across civilizations." *Ante*, at 3. For all those millennia, across all those civilizations, "marriage" referred to only one relationship: the union of a man and a woman. See *ante*, at 4; Tr. of Oral Arg. on Question 1, p. 12 (petitioners conceding that they are not aware of any society that permitted same-sex marriage before 2001). As the Court explained two Terms ago, "until recent years, . . . marriage between a man and a woman no doubt had been thought of by most people as essential to the very definition of that term and to its role and function throughout the history of civilization." *United States* v. *Windsor*, 570 U. S. ___, ___ (2013) (slip op., at 13).

This universal definition of marriage as the union of a man and a woman is no historical coincidence. Marriage did not come about as a result of a political movement, discovery, disease, war, religious doctrine, or any other moving force of world history—and certainly not as a result of a prehistoric decision to exclude gays and lesbians. It arose in the nature of things to meet a vital need: ensuring that children are conceived by a mother and father committed to raising them in the stable conditions of a lifelong relationship. See G. Quale, A History of Marriage Systems 2 (1988); cf. M. Cicero, De Officiis 57 (W. Miller transl. 1913) ("For since the reproductive instinct is by nature's gift the common possession of all living creatures, the first bond of union is that between husband and wife; the next, that between parents and children; then we find one home, with everything in common.").

The premises supporting this concept of marriage are so fundamental that they rarely require articulation. The human race must procreate to survive. Procreation occurs through sexual relations between a man and a woman. When sexual relations result in the conception of a child, that child's prospects are generally better if the mother and father stay together rather than going their separate ways. Therefore, for the good of children and society, sexual relations that can lead to procreation should occur only between a man and a woman committed to a lasting bond.

Society has recognized that bond as marriage. And by bestowing a respected status and material benefits on married couples, society encourages men and women to conduct sexual relations within marriage rather than without. As one prominent scholar put it, "Marriage is a socially arranged solution for the problem of getting people to stay together and care for children that the mere desire for children, and the sex that makes children possible, does not solve." J. Q. Wilson, The Marriage Problem 41 (2002).

This singular understanding of marriage has prevailed in the United States throughout our history. The majority accepts that at "the time of the Nation's founding [marriage] was understood to be a voluntary contract between a man and a woman." *Ante*, at 6. Early Americans drew heavily on legal scholars like William Blackstone, who regarded marriage between "husband and wife" as one of the "great relations in private life," and philosophers like John Locke, who described marriage as "a voluntary compact between man and woman" centered on "its chief end, procreation" and the "nourishment and support" of children. 1 W. Blackstone, Commentaries *410; J. Locke, Second Treatise of Civil Government §§78–79, p. 39 (J. Gough ed. 1947). To those who drafted and ratified the Constitution, this conception of marriage and family "was a given: its structure, its stability, roles, and values accepted by all." Forte, The Framers' Idea of Marriage and Family, in The Meaning of Marriage 100, 102 (R. George & J. Elshtain eds. 2006).

The Constitution itself says nothing about marriage, and the Framers thereby entrusted the States with "[t]he whole subject of the domestic relations of husband and wife." *Windsor*, 570 U. S., at ___ (slip op., at 17) (quoting *In re Burrus*, 136 U. S. 586, 593–594 (1890)). There is no dispute that every State at the founding—and every State throughout our history until a dozen years ago—defined marriage in the traditional, biologically rooted way. The four States in these cases are typical. Their laws, before and after statehood, have treated marriage as the union of a man and a woman. See *DeBoer* v. *Snyder*, 772 F. 3d 388, 396–399 (CA6 2014). Even when state laws did not spec- ify this definition expressly, no one doubted what they meant. See *Jones* v. *Hallahan*, 501 S. W. 2d 588, 589 (Ky. App. 1973). The meaning of "marriage" went without saying.

Of course, many did say it. In his first American dictionary, Noah Webster defined marriage as "the legal union of a man and woman for life," which served the purposes of "preventing the promiscuous intercourse of the sexes, . . . promoting domestic felicity, and . . . securing the maintenance and education of children." 1 An American Dictionary of the English Language (1828). An influential 19th-century treatise defined marriage as "a civil status, existing in one man and one woman legally united for life for those civil and social purposes which are based in the distinction of sex." J. Bishop, Commentaries on the Law of Marriage and Divorce 25 (1852). The first edition of Black's Law Dictionary defined marriage as "the civil status of one man and one woman united in law for life." Black's Law Dictionary 756 (1891) (emphasis deleted). The dictionary maintained essentially that same definition for the next century.

This Court's precedents have repeatedly described marriage in ways that are consistent only with its traditional meaning. Early cases on the subject referred to marriage as "the union for life of one man and one woman," *Murphy* v. *Ramsey*, 114 U. S. 15, 45 (1885), which forms "the foundation of the family and of society, without which there would be neither civilization nor progress," *Maynard* v. *Hill*, 125 U. S. 190, 211 (1888). We later described marriage as "fundamental to our very existence and survival," an understanding that necessarily implies a procreative component. *Loving* v. *Virginia*, 388 U. S. 1, 12 (1967); see *Skinner* v. *Oklahoma ex rel. Williamson*, 316 U. S. 535, 541 (1942). More recent cases have directly connected the right to marry with the "right to procreate." *Zablocki* v. *Redhail*, 434 U. S. 374, 386 (1978).

As the majority notes, some aspects of marriage have changed over time. Arranged marriages have largely given way to pairings based on romantic love. States have replaced coverture, the doctrine by which a married man and woman became a single legal entity, with laws that respect each participant's separate status. Racial restrictions on marriage, which "arose as an incident to slavery" to promote "White Supremacy," were repealed by many States and ultimately struck down by this Court.

Loving, 388 U. S., at 6–7.

The majority observes that these developments "were not mere superficial changes" in marriage, but rather "worked deep transformations in its structure." *Ante*, at 6–7. They did not, however, work any transformation in the core structure of marriage as the union between a man and a woman. If you had asked a person on the street how marriage was defined, no one would ever have said, "Marriage is the union of a man and a woman, where the woman is subject to coverture." The majority may be right that the "history of marriage is one of both continuity and change," but the core meaning of marriage has endured. *Ante*, at 6.

B

Shortly after this Court struck down racial restrictions on marriage in *Loving*, a gay couple in Minnesota sought a marriage license. They argued that the Constitution required States to allow marriage between people of the same sex for the same reasons that it requires States to allow marriage between people of different races. The Minnesota Supreme Court rejected their analogy to *Loving*, and this Court summarily dismissed an appeal. *Baker* v. *Nelson*, 409 U. S. 810 (1972).

In the decades after *Baker*, greater numbers of gays and lesbians began living openly, and many expressed a desire to have their relationships recognized as marriages. Over time, more people came to see marriage in a way that could be extended to such couples. Until recently, this new view of marriage remained a minority position. After the Massachusetts Supreme Judicial Court in 2003 interpreted its State Constitution to require recognition of same-sex marriage, many States—including the four at issue here—enacted constitutional amendments formally adopting the longstanding definition of marriage.

Over the last few years, public opinion on marriage has shifted rapidly. In 2009, the legislatures of Vermont, New Hampshire, and the District of Columbia became the first in the Nation to enact laws that revised the definition of marriage to include same-sex couples, while also providing accommodations for religious believers. In 2011, the New York Legislature enacted a similar law. In 2012, voters in Maine did the same, reversing the result of a referendum just three years earlier in which they had upheld the traditional definition of marriage.

In all, voters and legislators in eleven States and the District of Columbia have changed their definitions of marriage to include same-sex couples. The highest courts of five States have decreed that same result under their own Constitutions. The remainder of the States retain the traditional definition of marriage.

Petitioners brought lawsuits contending that the Due Process and Equal Protection Clauses of the Fourteenth Amendment compel their States to license and recognize marriages between same-sex couples. In a carefully reasoned decision, the Court of Appeals acknowledged the democratic "momentum" in favor of "expand[ing] the definition of marriage to include gay couples," but concluded that petitioners had not made "the case for constitutionalizing the definition of marriage and for removing the issue from the place it has been since the founding: in the hands of state voters." 772 F. 3d, at 396, 403. That decision interpreted the Constitution correctly, and I would affirm.

II

Petitioners first contend that the marriage laws of their States violate the Due Process Clause. The Solicitor General of the United States, appearing in support of petitioners, expressly disowned that position before this Court. See Tr. of Oral Arg. on Question 1, at 38–39. The majority nevertheless resolves these cases for petitioners based almost entirely on the Due Process Clause.

The majority purports to identify four "principles and traditions" in this Court's due process precedents that support a fundamental right for same-sex couples to marry. *Ante*, at 12. In reality, however, the majority's approach has no basis in principle or tradition, except for the unprincipled tradition of judicial policymaking that characterized discredited decisions such as *Lochner* v. *New York*, 198 U. S. 45. Stripped of its shiny rhetorical gloss, the majority's argument is that the Due Process Clause gives same-sex couples a fundamental right to marry because it will be good for them and for society. If I were a legislator, I would certainly consider that view as a matter of social policy. But as a judge, I find the majority's position indefensible as a matter of constitutional law.

A

Petitioners' "fundamental right" claim falls into the most sensitive category of constitutional adjudication. Petitioners do not contend that their States' marriage laws violate an *enumerated* constitutional right, such as the freedom of speech protected by the First Amendment. There is, after all, no "Companionship and Understanding" or "Nobility and Dignity" Clause in the Constitution. See *ante*, at 3, 14. They argue instead that the laws violate a right *implied* by the Fourteenth Amendment's requirement that "liberty" may not be deprived without "due process of law."

This Court has interpreted the Due Process Clause to include a "substantive" component that protects certain liberty interests against state deprivation "no matter what process is provided." *Reno* v. *Flores*, 507 U. S. 292, 302 (1993). The theory is that some liberties are "so rooted in the traditions and conscience of our people as to be ranked as fundamental," and therefore cannot be deprived without compelling justification. *Snyder* v. *Massachusetts*, 291 U. S. 97, 105 (1934).

Allowing unelected federal judges to select which unenumerated rights rank as "fundamental"—and to strike down state laws on the basis of that determination—raises obvious concerns about the judicial role. Our precedents have accordingly insisted that judges "exercise the utmost care" in identifying implied fundamental rights, "lest the liberty protected by the Due Process Clause be subtly transformed into the policy preferences of the Members of this Court." *Washington* v. *Glucksberg*, 521 U. S. 702, 720 (1997) (internal quotation marks omitted); see Kennedy, Unenumerated Rights and the Dictates of Judicial Restraint 13 (1986) (Address at Stanford) ("One can conclude that certain essential, or fundamental, rights should exist in any just society. It does not follow that each of those essential rights is one that we as judges can enforce under the written Constitution. The Due Process Clause is not a guarantee of every right that should inhere in an ideal system.").

The need for restraint in administering the strong medicine of substantive due process is a lesson this Court has learned the hard way. The Court first applied substantive due process to strike down a statute in *Dred Scott* v. *Sandford*, 19 How. 393 (1857). There the Court invalidated the Missouri Compromise on the ground that legislation restricting the institution of slavery violated the implied rights of slaveholders. The Court relied on its own conception of liberty and property in doing so. It asserted that "an act of Congress which deprives a citizen of the United States of his liberty or property, merely because he came himself or brought his property into a particular Territory of the United States . . . could hardly be dignified with the name of due process of law." *Id.,* at 450. In a dissent that has outlasted the majority opinion, Justice Curtis explained that when the "fixed rules which govern the interpretation of laws [are] abandoned, and the theoretical opinions of individuals are allowed to control" the Constitution's meaning, "we have no longer a Constitution; we are under the government of individual men, who for the time being have power to declare what the Constitution is, according to their own views of what it ought to mean." *Id.*, at 621.

Dred Scott's holding was overruled on the battlefields of the Civil War and by constitutional amendment after Appomattox, but its approach to the Due Process Clause reappeared. In a series of early 20th-century cases, most prominently *Lochner* v. *New York*, this Court invalidated state statutes that presented "meddlesome interferences with the rights of the individual," and "undue interference with liberty of person and freedom of contract." 198 U. S., at 60, 61. In *Lochner* itself, the Court struck down a New York law setting maximum hours for bakery employees, because there was "in our judgment, no reasonable foundation for holding this to be necessary or appropriate as a health law." *Id.,* at 58.

The dissenting Justices in *Lochner* explained that the New York law could be viewed as a reasonable response to legislative concern about the health of bakery employees, an issue on which there was at least "room for debate and for an honest difference of opinion." *Id.,* at 72 (opinion of Harlan, J.). The majority's contrary conclusion required adopting as constitutional law "an economic theory which a large part of the country does not entertain." *Id.,* at 75 (opinion of Holmes, J.). As Justice Holmes memorably put it, "The Fourteenth Amendment does not enact Mr. Herbert Spencer's Social Statics," a leading work on the philosophy of Social Darwinism. *Ibid.* The Constitution "is not intended to embody a particular economic theory . . . . It is made for people of fundamentally differing views, and the accident of our finding certain opinions natural and familiar or novel and even shocking ought not to conclude our judgment upon the question whether statutes embodying them conflict with the Constitution." *Id.*, at 75–76.

In the decades after *Lochner*, the Court struck down nearly 200 laws as violations of individual liberty, often over strong dissents contending that "[t]he criterion of constitutionality is not whether we believe the law to be for the public good." *Adkins* v. *Children's Hospital of D. C.*, 261 U. S. 525, 570 (1923) (opinion of Holmes, J.). By empowering judges to elevate their own policy judgments to the status of constitutionally protected "liberty," the

Lochner line of cases left "no alternative to regarding the court as a . . . legislative chamber." L. Hand, The Bill of Rights 42 (1958).

Eventually, the Court recognized its error and vowed not to repeat it. "The doctrine that . . . due process authorizes courts to hold laws unconstitutional when they believe the legislature has acted unwisely," we later explained, "has long since been discarded. We have returned to the original constitutional proposition that courts do not substitute their social and economic beliefs for the judgment of legislative bodies, who are elected to pass laws." *Ferguson* v. *Skrupa*, 372 U. S. 726, 730 (1963); see *DayBrite Lighting, Inc.* v. *Missouri*, 342 U. S. 421, 423 (1952) ("we do not sit as a super-legislature to weigh the wisdom of legislation"). Thus, it has become an accepted rule that the Court will not hold laws unconstitutional simply because we find them "unwise, improvident, or out of harmony with a particular school of thought." *Williamson* v. *Lee Optical of Okla., Inc.*, 348 U. S. 483, 488 (1955).

Rejecting *Lochner* does not require disavowing the doctrine of implied fundamental rights, and this Court has not done so. But to avoid repeating *Lochner*'s error of converting personal preferences into constitutional mandates, our modern substantive due process cases have stressed the need for "judicial self-restraint." *Collins* v. *Harker Heights*, 503 U. S. 115, 125 (1992). Our precedents have required that implied fundamental rights be "objectively, deeply rooted in this Nation's history and tradition," and "implicit in the concept of ordered liberty, such that neither liberty nor justice would exist if they were sacrificed." *Glucksberg*, 521 U. S., at 720–721 (internal quotation marks omitted).

Although the Court articulated the importance of his- tory and tradition to the fundamental rights inquiry most precisely in *Glucksberg*, many other cases both before and after have adopted the same approach. See, *e.g., District Attorney's Office for Third Judicial Dist.* v. *Osborne*, 557 U. S. 52, 72 (2009); *Flores*, 507 U. S., at 303; *United States* v. *Salerno*, 481 U. S. 739, 751 (1987); *Moore* v. *East Cleveland*, 431 U. S. 494, 503 (1977) (plurality opinion); see also *id.,* at 544 (White, J., dissenting) ("The Judiciary, including this Court, is the most vulnerable and comes nearest to illegitimacy when it deals with judge-made constitutional law having little or no cognizable roots in the language or even the design of the Constitution."); *Troxel* v. *Granville*, 530 U. S. 57, 96–101 (2000) (KENNEDY, J., dissenting) (consulting "'[o]ur Nation's history, legal traditions, and practices'" and concluding that "[w]e owe it to the Nation's domestic relations legal structure . . . to proceed with caution" (quoting *Glucksberg*, 521 U. S., at 721)).

Proper reliance on history and tradition of course requires looking beyond the individual law being challenged, so that every restriction on liberty does not supply its own constitutional justification. The Court is right about that. *Ante*, at 18. But given the few "guideposts for responsible decisionmaking in this unchartered area," *Collins*, 503 U. S., at 125, "an approach grounded in history imposes limits on the judiciary that are more meaningful than any based on [an] abstract formula," *Moore*, 431 U. S., at 504, n. 12 (plurality opinion). Expanding a right suddenly and dramatically is likely to require tearing it up from its roots. Even a sincere profession of "discipline" in identifying fundamental rights, *ante*, at 10–11, does not provide a meaningful constraint on a judge, for "what he is really likely to be 'discovering,' whether or not he is fully aware of it, are his own values," J. Ely, Democracy and Distrust 44 (1980). The only way to ensure restraint in this delicate enterprise is "continual insistence upon respect for the teachings of history, solid recognition of the basic values that underlie our society, and wise appreciation of the great roles [of] the doctrines of federalism and separation of powers." *Griswold* v. *Connecticut*, 381 U. S. 479, 501 (1965) (Harlan, J., concurring in judgment).

B

The majority acknowledges none of this doctrinal background, and it is easy to see why: Its aggressive application of substantive due process breaks sharply with decades of precedent and returns the Court to the unprincipled approach of *Lochner*.

1

The majority's driving themes are that marriage is desirable and petitioners desire it. The opinion describes the "transcendent importance" of marriage and repeatedly insists that petitioners do not seek to "demean," "devalue," "denigrate," or "disrespect" the institution. *Ante*, at 3, 4, 6, 28. Nobody disputes those points. Indeed, the compelling personal accounts of petitioners and others like them are likely a primary reason why many Americans have changed their minds about whether same-sex couples should be allowed to marry. As a matter of constitutional law, however, the sincerity of petitioners' wishes is not relevant.

When the majority turns to the law, it relies primarily on precedents discussing the fundamental "right to marry." *Turner* v. *Safley*, 482 U. S. 78, 95 (1987); *Zablocki*, 434 U. S., at 383; see *Loving*, 388 U. S., at 12. These cases do not hold, of course, that anyone who wants to get married has a constitutional right to do so. They instead require a State to justify barriers to marriage as that institution has always been understood. In *Loving*, the Court held that racial restrictions on the right to marry lacked a compelling justification. In *Zablocki*, restrictions based on child support debts did not suffice. In *Turner*, restrictions based on status as a prisoner were deemed impermissible.

None of the laws at issue in those cases purported to change the core definition of marriage as the union of a man and a woman. The laws challenged in *Zablocki* and *Turner* did not define marriage as "the union of a man and a woman, *where neither party owes child support or is in prison.*" Nor did the interracial marriage ban at issue in *Loving* define marriage as "the union of a man and a woman *of the same race.*" See Tragen, Comment, Statutory Prohibitions Against Interracial Marriage, 32 Cal. L. Rev. 269 (1944) ("at common law there was no ban on interracial marriage"); *post*, at 11–12, n. 5 (THOMAS, J., dissenting). Removing racial barriers to marriage therefore did not change what a marriage was any more than integrating schools changed what a school was. As the majority admits, the institution of "marriage" discussed in every one of these cases "presumed a relationship involving opposite-sex partners." *Ante*, at 11.

In short, the "right to marry" cases stand for the important but limited proposition that particular restrictions on access to marriage *as traditionally defined* violate due process. These precedents say nothing at all about a right to make a State change its definition of marriage, which is the right petitioners actually seek here. See *Windsor*, 570 U. S., at ___ (ALITO, J., dissenting) (slip op., at 8) ("What Windsor and the United States seek . . . is not the protection of a deeply rooted right but the recognition of a very new right."). Neither petitioners nor the majority cites a single case or other legal source providing any basis for such a constitutional right. None exists, and that is enough to foreclose their claim.

2

The majority suggests that "there are other, more instructive precedents" informing the right to marry. *Ante*, at 12. Although not entirely clear, this reference seems to correspond to a line of cases discussing an implied fundamental "right of privacy." *Griswold*, 381 U. S., at 486. In the first of those cases, the Court invalidated a criminal law that banned the use of contraceptives. *Id.*, at 485– 486. The Court stressed the invasive nature of the ban, which threatened the intrusion of "the police to search the sacred precincts of marital bedrooms." *Id.,* at 485. In the Court's view, such laws infringed the right to privacy in its most basic sense: the "right to be let alone." *Eisenstadt* v. *Baird*, 405 U. S. 438, 453–454, n. 10 (1972) (internal quotation marks omitted); see *Olmstead* v. *United States*, 277 U. S. 438, 478 (1928) (Brandeis, J., dissenting).

The Court also invoked the right to privacy in *Lawrence* v. *Texas*, 539 U. S. 558 (2003), which struck down a Texas statute criminalizing homosexual sodomy. *Lawrence* relied on the position that criminal sodomy laws, like bans on contraceptives, invaded privacy by inviting "unwarranted government intrusions" that "touc[h] upon the most private human conduct, sexual behavior . . . in the most private of places, the home." *Id.*, at 562, 567.

Neither *Lawrence* nor any other precedent in the privacy line of cases supports the right that petitioners assert here. Unlike criminal laws banning contraceptives and sodomy, the marriage laws at issue here involve no government intrusion. They create no crime and impose no punishment. Same-sex couples remain free to live together, to engage in intimate conduct, and to raise their fami- lies as they see fit. No one is "condemned to live in loneliness" by the laws challenged in these cases—no one. *Ante*, at 28. At the same time, the laws in no way interfere with the "right to be let alone."

The majority also relies on Justice Harlan's influential dissenting opinion in *Poe* v. *Ullman*, 367 U. S. 497 (1961). As the majority recounts, that opinion states that "[d]ue process has not been reduced to any formula." *Id.,* at 542. But far from conferring the broad interpretive discretion that the majority discerns, Justice Harlan's opinion makes clear that courts implying fundamental rights are not "free to roam where unguided speculation might take them." *Ibid.* They must instead have "regard to what history teaches" and exercise not only "judgment" but "restraint." *Ibid.* Of particular relevance, Justice Harlan explained that "laws regarding marriage which provide both when the sexual powers may be used and the legal and societal context in which children are born and brought up . . . form a pattern so deeply pressed into the substance of our social life that any Constitutional doctrine in this area must build upon that basis." *Id.*, at 546.

In sum, the privacy cases provide no support for the majority's position, because petitioners do not seek pri- vacy. Quite the opposite, they seek public recognition of their relationships, along with corresponding government benefits. Our cases have consistently refused to allow litigants to convert the shield provided by constitutional liberties into a sword to demand positive entitlements from the State. See *DeShaney* v. *Winnebago County Dept. of Social Servs.*, 489 U. S. 189, 196 (1989); *San Antonio Independent School Dist.* v. *Rodriguez*, 411 U. S. 1, 35–37 (1973); *post*, at 9–13 (THOMAS, J., dissenting). Thus, although the right to privacy recognized by our precedents certainly plays a role in protecting the intimate conduct of same-sex couples, it provides no affirmative right to redefine marriage and no basis for striking down the laws at issue here.

3

Perhaps recognizing how little support it can derive from precedent, the majority goes out of its way to jettison the "careful" approach to implied fundamental rights taken by this Court in *Glucksberg*. *Ante*, at 18 (quoting 521 U. S., at 721). It is revealing that the majority's position requires it to effectively overrule *Glucksberg*, the leading modern case setting the bounds of substantive due process. At least this part of the majority opinion has the virtue of candor. Nobody could rightly accuse the majority of taking a careful approach.

Ultimately, only one precedent offers any support for the majority's methodology: *Lochner* v. *New York*, 198 U. S. 45. The majority opens its opinion by announcing petitioners' right to "define and express their identity." *Ante*, at 1–2. The majority later explains that "the right to personal choice regarding marriage is inherent in the concept of individual autonomy." *Ante*, at 12. This freewheeling notion of individual autonomy echoes nothing so much as "the general right of an individual to be *free in his person* and in his power to contract in relation to his own labor." *Lochner*, 198 U. S., at 58 (emphasis added).

To be fair, the majority does not suggest that its individual autonomy right is entirely unconstrained. The constraints it sets are precisely those that accord with its own "reasoned judgment," informed by its "new insight" into the "nature of injustice," which was invisible to all who came before but has become clear "as we learn [the] meaning" of liberty. *Ante*, at 10, 11. The truth is that today's decision rests on nothing more than the majority's own conviction that same-sex couples should be allowed to marry because they want to, and that "it would disparage their choices and diminish their personhood to deny them this right." *Ante*, at 19. Whatever force that belief may have as a matter of moral philosophy, it has no more basis in the Constitution than did the naked policy preferences adopted in *Lochner*. See 198 U. S., at 61 ("We do not believe in the soundness of the views which uphold this law," which "is an illegal interference with the rights of individuals . . . to make contracts regarding labor upon such terms as they may think best").

The majority recognizes that today's cases do not mark "the first time the Court has been asked to adopt a cautious approach to recognizing and protecting fundamental rights." *Ante*, at 25. On that much, we agree. The Court was "asked"—and it agreed—to "adopt a cautious approach" to implying fundamental rights after the debacle of the *Lochner* era. Today, the majority casts caution aside and revives the grave errors of that period.

One immediate question invited by the majority's position is whether States may retain the definition of marriage as a union of two people. Cf. *Brown* v. *Buhman*, 947 F. Supp. 2d 1170 (Utah 2013), appeal pending, No. 14-4117 (CA10). Although the majority randomly inserts the adjective "two" in various places, it offers no reason at all why the two-person element of the core definition of marriage may be preserved while the man-woman element may not. Indeed, from the standpoint of history and tradition, a leap from opposite-sex marriage to same-sex marriage is much greater than one from a two-person union to plural unions, which have deep roots in some cultures around the world. If the majority is willing to take the big leap, it is hard to see how it can say no to the shorter one.

It is striking how much of the majority's reasoning would apply with equal force to the claim of a fundamental right to plural marriage. If "[t]here is dignity in the bond between two men or two women who seek to marry and in their autonomy to make such profound choices," *ante*, at 13, why would there be any less dignity in the bond between three people who, in exercising their autonomy, seek to make the profound choice to marry? If a same-sex couple has the constitutional right to marry because their children would otherwise "suffer the stigma of knowing their families are somehow lesser," *ante*, at 15, why wouldn't the same reasoning apply to a family of three or more persons raising children? If not having the opportunity to marry "serves to disrespect and subordinate" gay and lesbian couples, why wouldn't the same "imposition of this disability," *ante*, at 22, serve to disrespect and subordinate people who find fulfillment in polyamorous relationships? See Bennett, Polyamory: The Next Sexual Revolution? Newsweek, July 28, 2009 (estimating 500,000 polyamorous families in the United States); Li, Married Lesbian "Throuple" Expecting First Child, N. Y. Post, Apr. 23, 2014; Otter, Three May Not Be a Crowd: The Case for a Constitutional Right to Plural Marriage, 64 Emory L. J. 1977 (2015).

I do not mean to equate marriage between same-sex couples with plural marriages in all respects. There may well be relevant differences that compel different legal analysis. But if there are, petitioners have not pointed to any. When asked about a plural marital union at oral argument, petitioners asserted that a State "doesn't have such an institution." Tr. of Oral Arg. on Question 2, p. 6. But that is exactly the point: the States at issue here do not have an institution of same-sex marriage, either.

4

Near the end of its opinion, the majority offers perhaps the clearest insight into its decision. Expanding marriage to include same-sex couples, the majority insists, would "pose no risk of harm to themselves or third parties." *Ante*, at 27. This argument again echoes *Lochner*, which relied on its assessment that "we think that a law like the one before us involves neither the safety, the morals nor the welfare of the public, and that the interest of the public is not in the slightest degree affected by such an act." 198 U. S., at 57.

Then and now, this assertion of the "harm principle" sounds more in philosophy than law. The elevation of the fullest individual self-realization over the constraints that society has expressed in law may or may not be attractive moral philosophy. But a Justice's commission does not confer any special moral, philosophical, or social insight sufficient to justify imposing those perceptions on fellow citizens under the pretense of "due process." There is indeed a process due the people on issues of this sort—the democratic process. Respecting that understanding requires the Court to be guided by law, not any particular school of social thought. As Judge Henry Friendly once put it, echoing Justice Holmes's dissent in *Lochner*, the Fourteenth Amendment does not enact John Stuart Mill's On Liberty any more than it enacts Herbert Spencer's Social Statics. See Randolph, Before *Roe v. Wade*: Judge Friendly's Draft Abortion Opinion, 29 Harv. J. L. & Pub. Pol'y 1035, 1036–1037, 1058 (2006). And it certainly does not enact any one concept of marriage.

The majority's understanding of due process lays out a tantalizing vision of the future for Members of this Court: If an unvarying social institution enduring over all of recorded history cannot inhibit judicial policymaking, what can? But this approach is dangerous for the rule of law. The purpose of insisting that implied fundamental rights have roots in the history and tradition of our people is to ensure that when unelected judges strike down democratically enacted laws, they do so based on something more than their own beliefs. The Court today not only overlooks our country's entire history and tradition but actively repudiates it, preferring to live only in the heady days of the here and now. I agree with the majority that the "nature of injustice is that we may not always see it in our own times." *Ante*, at 11. As petitioners put it, "times can blind." Tr. of Oral Arg. on Question 1, at 9, 10. But to blind yourself to history is both prideful and unwise. "The past is never dead. It's not even past." W. Faulkner, Requiem for a Nun 92 (1951).

III

In addition to their due process argument, petitioners contend that the Equal Protection Clause requires their States to license and recognize same-sex marriages. The majority does not seriously engage with this claim. Its discussion is, quite frankly, difficult to follow. The central point seems to be that there is a "synergy between" the Equal Protection Clause and the Due Process Clause, and that some precedents relying on one Clause have also relied on the other. *Ante*, at 20. Absent from this portion of the opinion, however, is anything resembling our usual framework for deciding equal protection cases. It is casebook doctrine that the "modern Supreme Court's treatment of equal protection claims has used a means-ends methodology in which judges ask whether the classification the government is using is sufficiently related to the goals it is pursuing." G. Stone, L. Seidman, C. Sunstein, M. Tushnet, & P. Karlan, Constitutional Law 453 (7th ed. 2013). The majority's approach today is different:

> "Rights implicit in liberty and rights secured by equal protection may rest on different precepts and are not always co-extensive, yet in some instances each may be instructive as to the meaning and reach of the other. In any particular case one Clause may be thought to capture the essence of the right in a more accurate and comprehensive way, even as the two Clauses may converge in the identification and definition of the right." *Ante*, at 19.

The majority goes on to assert in conclusory fashion that the Equal Protection Clause provides an alternative basis for its holding. *Ante*, at 22. Yet the majority fails to provide even a single sentence explaining how the Equal Protection Clause supplies independent weight for its position, nor does it attempt to justify its gratuitous violation of the canon against unnecessarily resolving constitutional questions. See *Northwest Austin Municipal Util. Dist. No. One* v. *Holder*, 557 U. S. 193, 197 (2009). In any event, the marriage laws at issue here do not violate the Equal Protection Clause, because distinguishing between opposite-sex and same-sex couples is rationally related to the States' "legitimate state interest" in "preserving the traditional institution of marriage." *Lawrence*, 539 U. S., at 585 (O'Connor, J., concurring in judgment).

It is important to note with precision which laws petitioners have challenged. Although they discuss some of the ancillary legal benefits that accompany marriage, such as hospital visitation rights and recognition of spousal status on official documents, petitioners' lawsuits target the laws defining marriage generally rather than those allocating benefits specifically. The equal protection analysis might be different, in my view, if we were confronted with a more focused challenge to the denial of certain tangible benefits. Of course, those more selective claims will not arise now that the Court has taken the drastic step of requiring every State to license and recognize marriages between same-sex couples.

IV

The legitimacy of this Court ultimately rests "upon the respect accorded to its judgments." *Republican Party of Minn.* v. *White*, 536 U. S. 765, 793 (2002) (KENNEDY, J., concurring). That respect flows from the perception—and reality—that we exercise humility and restraint in deciding cases according to the Constitution and law. The role of the Court envisioned by the majority today, however, is anything but humble or restrained. Over and over, the majority exalts the role of the judiciary in delivering social change. In the majority's telling, it is the courts, not the people, who are responsible for making "new dimensions of freedom . . . apparent to new generations," for providing "formal discourse" on social issues, and for ensuring "neutral discussions, without scornful or disparaging commentary." *Ante*, at 7–9.

Nowhere is the majority's extravagant conception of judicial supremacy more evident than in its description— and dismissal—of the public debate regarding same-sex marriage. Yes, the majority concedes, on one side are thousands of years of human history in every society known to have populated the planet. But on the other side, there has been "extensive litigation," "many thoughtful District Court decisions," "countless studies, papers, books, and other popular and scholarly writings," and "more than 100" *amicus* briefs in these cases alone. *Ante*, at 9, 10, 23. What would be the point of allowing the democratic process to go on? It is high time for the Court to decide the meaning of marriage, based on five lawyers' "better informed understanding" of "a liberty that remains urgent in our own era." *Ante*, at 19. The answer is surely there in one of those *amicus* briefs or studies.

Those who founded our country would not recognize the majority's conception of the judicial role. They after all risked their lives and fortunes for the precious right to govern themselves. They would never have imagined yielding that right on a question of social policy to unaccountable and unelected judges. And they certainly would not have been satisfied by a system empowering judges to override policy judgments so long as they do so after "a quite extensive discussion." *Ante*, at 8. In our democracy, debate about the content of the law is not an exhaustion requirement to be checked off before courts can impose their will. "Surely the Constitution does not put either the legislative branch or the executive branch in the position of a television quiz show contestant so that when a given period of time has elapsed and a problem remains unresolved by them, the federal judiciary may press a buzzer and take its turn at fashioning a solution." Rehnquist, The Notion of a Living Constitution, 54 Texas L. Rev. 693, 700 (1976). As a plurality of this Court explained just last year, "It is demeaning to the democratic process to presume that voters are not capable of deciding an issue of this sensitivity on decent and rational grounds." *Schuette* v. *BAMN*, 572 U. S. ___, ___ –___ (2014) (slip op., at 16– 17).

The Court's accumulation of power does not occur in a vacuum. It comes at the expense of the people. And they know it. Here and abroad, people are in the midst of a serious and thoughtful public debate on the issue of same-sex marriage. They see voters carefully considering same-sex marriage, casting ballots in favor or opposed, and sometimes changing their minds. They see political leaders similarly reexamining their positions, and either reversing course or explaining adherence to old convictions confirmed anew. They see governments and businesses modifying policies and practices with respect to same-sex couples, and participating actively in the civic discourse. They see countries overseas democratically accepting profound social change, or declining to do so. This deliberative process is making people take seriously questions that they may not have even regarded as questions before.

When decisions are reached through democratic means, some people will inevitably be disappointed with the results. But those whose views do not prevail at least know that they have had their say, and accordingly are—in the tradition of our political culture—reconciled to the result of a fair and honest debate. In addition, they can gear up to raise the issue later, hoping to persuade enough on the winning side to think again. "That is exactly how our system of government is supposed to work." *Post,* at 2–3 (SCALIA, J., dissenting).

But today the Court puts a stop to all that. By deciding this question under the Constitution, the Court removes it from the realm of democratic decision. There will be consequences to shutting down the political process on an issue of such profound public significance. Closing debate tends to close minds. People denied a voice are less likely to accept the ruling of a court on an issue that does not seem to be the sort of thing courts usually decide. As a thoughtful commentator observed about another issue, "The political process was moving . . . , not swiftly enough for advocates of quick, complete change, but majoritarian institutions were listening and acting. Heavy-handed judicial intervention was difficult to justify and appears to have provoked, not resolved, conflict." Ginsburg, Some Thoughts on Autonomy and Equality in Relation to *Roe v. Wade*, 63 N. C. L. Rev. 375, 385–386 (1985) (footnote omitted). Indeed, however heartened the proponents of same-sex marriage might be on this day, it is worth acknowledging what they have lost, and lost forever: the opportunity to win the true acceptance that comes from persuading their fellow citizens of the justice of their cause. And they lose this just when the winds of change were freshening at their backs.

Federal courts are blunt instruments when it comes to creating rights. They have constitutional power only to resolve concrete cases or controversies; they do not have the flexibility of legislatures to address concerns of parties not before the court or to anticipate problems that may arise from the exercise of a new right. Today's decision, for example, creates serious questions about religious liberty. Many good and decent people oppose same-sex marriage as a tenet of faith, and their freedom to exercise religion is—unlike the right imagined by the majority— actually spelled out in the Constitution. Amdt. 1.

Respect for sincere religious conviction has led voters and legislators in every State that has adopted same-sex marriage democratically to include accommodations for religious practice. The majority's decision imposing same-sex marriage cannot, of course, create any such accommodations. The majority graciously suggests that religious believers may continue to "advocate" and "teach" their views of marriage. *Ante*, at 27. The First Amendment guarantees, however, the freedom to "*exercise*" religion. Ominously, that is not a word the majority uses.

Hard questions arise when people of faith exercise religion in ways that may be seen to conflict with the new right to same-sex marriage—when, for example, a religious college provides married student housing only to opposite-sex married couples, or a religious adoption agency declines to place children with same-sex married couples. Indeed, the Solicitor General candidly acknowledged that the tax exemptions of some religious institutions would be in question if they opposed same-sex marriage. See Tr. of Oral Arg. on Question 1, at 36–38. There is little doubt that these and similar questions will soon be before this Court. Unfortunately, people of faith can take no comfort in the treatment they receive from the majority today.

Perhaps the most discouraging aspect of today's decision is the extent to which the majority feels compelled to sully those on the other side of the debate. The majority offers a cursory assurance that it does not intend to disparage people who, as a matter of conscience, cannot accept same-sex marriage. *Ante*, at 19. That disclaimer is hard to square with the very next sentence, in which the majority explains that "the necessary consequence" of laws codifying the traditional definition of marriage is to "demea[n] or stigmatiz[e]" same-sex couples. *Ante*, at 19. The majority reiterates such characterizations over and over. By the majority's account, Americans who did nothing more than follow the understanding of marriage that has existed for our entire history—in particular, the tens of millions of people who voted to reaffirm their States' enduring definition of marriage—have acted to "lock . . . out," "disparage," "disrespect and subordinate," and inflict "[d]ignitary wounds" upon their gay and lesbian neighbors. *Ante*, at 17, 19, 22, 25. These apparent assaults on the character of fairminded people will have an effect, in society and in court. See *post*, at 6–7 (AUITO, J., dissenting). Moreover, they are entirely gratuitous. It is one thing for the majority to conclude that the Constitution protects a right to same-sex marriage; it is something else to portray everyone who does not share the majority's "better informed understanding" as bigoted. *Ante*, at 19.

In the face of all this, a much different view of the Court's role is possible. That view is more modest and restrained. It is more skeptical that the legal abilities of judges also reflect insight into moral and philosophical issues. It is more sensitive to the fact that judges are unelected and unaccountable, and that the legitimacy of their power depends on confining it to the exercise of legal judgment. It is more attuned to the lessons of history, and what it has meant for the country and Court when Justices have exceeded their proper bounds. And it is less pretentious than to suppose that while people around the world have viewed an institution in a particular way for thousands of years, the present generation and the present Court are the ones chosen to burst the bonds of that history and tradition.

* * *

If you are among the many Americans—of whatever sexual orientation—who favor expanding same-sex marriage, by all means celebrate today's decision. Celebrate the achievement of a desired goal. Celebrate the opportunity for a new expression of commitment to a partner. Celebrate the availability of new benefits. But do not celebrate the Constitution. It had nothing to do with it.

I respectfully dissent.

Scalia, J., Dissenting

SUPREME COURT OF THE UNITED STATES

Nos. 14–556, 14-562, 14-571 and 14–574
JAMES OBERGEFELL, ET AL., PETITIONERS
14–556 *v.*
RICHARD HODGES, DIRECTOR, OHIO
DEPARTMENT OF HEALTH, ET AL.;
VALERIA TANCO, ET AL., PETITIONERS
14–562 *v.*
BILL HASLAM, GOVERNOR OF
TENNESSEE, ET AL.;
APRIL DEBOER, ET AL., PETITIONERS
14–571 *v.*
RICK SNYDER, GOVERNOR OF MICHIGAN,
ET AL.; AND
GREGORY BOURKE, ET AL., PETITIONERS
14–574 *v.*
STEVE BESHEAR, GOVERNOR OF
KENTUCKY

ON WRITS OF CERTIORARI TO THE UNITED STATES COURT OF APPEALS FOR THE SIXTH CIRCUIT
[June 26, 2015]

JUSTICE SCALIA, with whom JUSTICE THOMAS joins, dissenting.

I join THE CHIEF JUSTICE's opinion in full. I write separately to call attention to this Court's threat to American democracy.

The substance of today's decree is not of immense personal importance to me. The law can recognize as marriage whatever sexual attachments and living arrangements it wishes, and can accord them favorable civil consequences, from tax treatment to rights of inheritance.

Those civil consequences—and the public approval that conferring the name of marriage evidences—can perhaps have adverse social effects, but no more adverse than the effects of many other controversial laws. So it is not of special importance to me what the law says about marriage. It is of overwhelming importance, however, who it is that rules me. Today's decree says that my Ruler, and the Ruler of 320 million Americans coast-to-coast, is a majority of the nine lawyers on the Supreme Court. The opinion in these cases is the furthest extension in fact— and the furthest extension one can even imagine—of the Court's claimed power to create "liberties" that the Constitution and its Amendments neglect to mention. This practice of constitutional revision by an unelected committee of nine, always accompanied (as it is today) by extravagant praise of liberty, robs the People of the most important liberty they asserted in the Declaration of Independence and won in the Revolution of 1776: the freedom to govern themselves.

I

Until the courts put a stop to it, public debate over same-sex marriage displayed American democracy at its best. Individuals on both sides of the issue passionately, but respectfully, attempted to persuade their fellow citizens to accept their views. Americans considered the arguments and put the question to a vote. The electorates of 11 States, either directly or through their representatives, chose to expand the traditional definition of marriage. Many more decided not to.[1] Win or lose, advocates for both sides continued pressing their cases, secure in the knowledge that an electoral loss can be negated by a later electoral win. That is exactly how our system of government is supposed to work.[2]

The Constitution places some constraints on self-rule— constraints adopted *by the People themselves* when they ratified the Constitution and its Amendments. Forbidden are laws "impairing the Obligation of Contracts,"[3] denying "Full Faith and Credit" to the "public Acts" of other States,[4] prohibiting the free exercise of religion,[5] abridging the freedom of speech,[6] infringing the right to keep and bear arms,[7] authorizing unreasonable searches and seizures,[8] and so forth. Aside from these limitations, those powers "reserved to the States respectively, or to the people"[9] can be exercised as the States or the People desire. These cases ask us to decide whether the Fourteenth Amendment contains a limitation that requires the States to license and recognize marriages between two people of the same sex. Does it remove *that* issue from the political process?

Of course not. It would be surprising to find a prescription regarding marriage in the Federal Constitution since, as the author of today's opinion reminded us only two years ago (in an opinion joined by the same Justices who join him today):

> "[R]egulation of domestic relations is an area that has long been regarded as a virtually exclusive province of the States."[10]
>
> "[T]he Federal Government, through our history, has deferred to state-law policy decisions with respect to domestic relations."[11]

But we need not speculate. When the Fourteenth Amendment was ratified in 1868, every State limited marriage to one man and one woman, and no one doubted the constitutionality of doing so. That resolves these cases. When it comes to determining the meaning of a vague constitutional provision—such as "due process of law" or "equal protection of the laws"—it is unquestionable that the People who ratified that provision did not understand it to prohibit a practice that remained both universal and uncontroversial in the years after ratification.[12] We have no basis for striking down a practice that is not expressly prohibited by the Fourteenth Amendment's text, and that bears the endorsement of a long tradition of open, widespread, and unchallenged use dating back to the Amendment's ratification. Since there is no doubt whatever that the People never decided to prohibit the limitation of marriage to opposite-sex couples, the public debate over same-sex marriage must be allowed to continue.

But the Court ends this debate, in an opinion lacking even a thin veneer of law. Buried beneath the mummeries and straining-to-be-memorable passages of the opinion is a candid and startling assertion: No matter *what* it was the

People ratified, the Fourteenth Amendment protects those rights that the Judiciary, in its "reasoned judgment," thinks the Fourteenth Amendment ought to protect.[13] That is so because "[t]he generations that wrote and ratified the Bill of Rights and the Fourteenth Amendment did not presume to know the extent of freedom in all of its dimensions . . . ."[14] One would think that sentence would continue: ". . . and therefore they provided for a means by which the People could amend the Constitution," or perhaps ". . . and therefore they left the creation of additional liberties, such as the freedom to marry someone of the same sex, to the People, through the never-ending process of legislation." But no. What logically follows, in the majority's judge-empowering estimation, is: "and so they entrusted to future generations a charter protecting the right of all persons to enjoy liberty as we learn its meaning."[15] The "we," needless to say, is the nine of us. "History and tradition guide and discipline [our] inquiry but do not set its outer boundaries."[16] Thus, rather than focusing on *the People's* understanding of "liberty"—at the time of ratification or even today—the majority focuses on four "principles and traditions" that, *in the majority's view*, prohibit States from defining marriage as an institution consisting of one man and one woman.[17]

This is a naked judicial claim to legislative—indeed, *super*-legislative—power; a claim fundamentally at odds with our system of government. Except as limited by a constitutional prohibition agreed to by the People, the States are free to adopt whatever laws they like, even those that offend the esteemed Justices' "reasoned judgment." A system of government that makes the People subordinate to a committee of nine unelected lawyers does not deserve to be called a democracy.

Judges are selected precisely for their skill as lawyers; whether they reflect the policy views of a particular constituency is not (or should not be) relevant. Not surprisingly then, the Federal Judiciary is hardly a cross-section of America. Take, for example, this Court, which consists of only nine men and women, all of them successful lawyers[18] who studied at Harvard or Yale Law School. Four of the nine are natives of New York City. Eight of them grew up in east- and west-coast States. Only one hails from the vast expanse in-between. Not a single Southwesterner or even, to tell the truth, a genuine Westerner (California does not count). Not a single evangelical Christian (a group that comprises about one quarter of Americans[19]), or even a Protestant of any denomination. The strikingly unrepresentative character of the body voting on today's social upheaval would be irrelevant if they were functioning as *judges*, answering the legal question whether the American people had ever ratified a constitutional provision that was understood to proscribe the traditional definition of marriage. But of course the Justices in today's majority are not voting on that basis; *they say they are not*. And to allow the policy question of same-sex marriage to be considered and resolved by a select, patrician, highly unrepresentative panel of nine is to violate a principle even more fundamental than no taxation without representation: no social transformation without representation.

II

But what really astounds is the hubris reflected in today's judicial Putsch. The five Justices who compose today's majority are entirely comfortable concluding that every State violated the Constitution for all of the 135 years between the Fourteenth Amendment's ratification and Massachusetts' permitting of same-sex marriages in 2003.[20] They have discovered in the Fourteenth Amendment a "fundamental right" overlooked by every person alive at the time of ratification, and almost everyone else in the time since. They see what lesser legal minds— minds like Thomas Cooley, John Marshall Harlan, Oliver Wendell Holmes, Jr., Learned Hand, Louis Brandeis, William Howard Taft, Benjamin Cardozo, Hugo Black, Felix Frankfurter, Robert Jackson, and Henry Friendly— could not. They are certain that the People ratified the Fourteenth Amendment to bestow on them the power to remove questions from the democratic process when that is called for by their "reasoned judgment." These Justices *know* that limiting marriage to one man and one woman is contrary to reason; they *know* that an institution as old as government itself, and accepted by every nation in history until 15 years ago,[21] cannot possibly be supported by anything other than ignorance or bigotry. And they are willing to say that any citizen who does not agree with that, who adheres to what was, until 15 years ago, the unanimous judgment of all generations and all societies, stands against the Constitution.

The opinion is couched in a style that is as pretentious as its content is egotistic. It is one thing for separate concurring or dissenting opinions to contain extravagances, even silly extravagances, of thought and expression; it is something else for the official opinion of the Court to do so.[22] Of course the opinion's showy profundities are often profoundly incoherent. "The nature of marriage is that, through its enduring bond, two persons together can find other freedoms, such as expression, intimacy, and spirituality."[23] (Really? Who ever thought that intimacy and spirituality [whatever that means] were freedoms? And if intimacy is, one would think Freedom of Intimacy is abridged rather than expanded by marriage. Ask the nearest hippie. Expression, sure enough, *is* a freedom, but anyone in a long-lasting marriage will attest that that happy state constricts, rather than expands, what one can prudently say.) Rights, we are told, can "rise . . . from a better informed understanding of how constitutional imperatives define a liberty that remains urgent in our own era."[24] (Huh? How can a better informed understanding of how constitutional imperatives [whatever that means] define [whatever that means] an urgent liberty [never mind], give birth to a right?) And we are told that, "[i]n any particular case," either the Equal Protection or Due Process Clause "may be thought to capture the essence of [a] right in a more accurate and comprehensive way," than the other, "even as the two Clauses may converge in the identification and definition of the right."[25] (What say? What possible "essence" does substantive due process "capture" in an "accurate and comprehensive way"? It stands for nothing whatever, except those freedoms and entitlements that this Court *really* likes. And the Equal Protection Clause, as employed today, identifies nothing except a difference in treatment that this Court *really* dislikes. Hardly a distillation of essence. If the opinion is correct that the two clauses "converge in the identification and definition of [a] right," that is only because the majority's likes and dislikes are predictably compatible.) I could go on. The world does not expect logic and precision in poetry or inspirational pop-philosophy; it demands them in the law. The stuff contained in today's opinion has to diminish this Court's reputation for clear thinking and sober analysis.

* * *

Hubris is sometimes defined as o'erweening pride; and pride, we know, goeth before a fall. The Judiciary is the "least dangerous" of the federal branches because it has "neither Force nor Will, but merely judgment; and must ultimately depend upon the aid of the executive arm" and the States, "even for the efficacy of its judgments."[26] With each decision of ours that takes from the People a question properly left to them—with each decision that is unabashedly based not on law, but on the "reasoned judgment" of a bare majority of this Court—we move one step closer to being reminded of our impotence.

THOMAS, J., DISSENTING

SUPREME COURT OF THE UNITED STATES

Nos. 14–556, 14-562, 14-571 and 14–574

JAMES OBERGEFELL, ET AL., PETITIONERS

14–556 *v.*

RICHARD HODGES, DIRECTOR, OHIO DEPARTMENT OF HEALTH, ET AL.;

VALERIA TANCO, ET AL., PETITIONERS

14–562 *v.*

BILL HASLAM, GOVERNOR OF TENNESSEE, ET AL.;

APRIL DEBOER, ET AL., PETITIONERS

14–571 *v.*

RICK SNYDER, GOVERNOR OF MICHIGAN, ET AL.; AND

GREGORY BOURKE, ET AL., PETITIONERS

14–574 *v.*

STEVE BESHEAR, GOVERNOR OF KENTUCKY

ON WRITS OF CERTIORARI TO THE UNITED STATES COURT OF APPEALS FOR THE SIXTH CIRCUIT

[June 26, 2015]

JUSTICE THOMAS, with whom JUSTICE SCALIA joins, dissenting.

The Court's decision today is at odds not only with the Constitution, but with the principles upon which our Nation was built. Since well before 1787, liberty has been understood as freedom from government action, not entitlement to government benefits. The Framers created our Constitution to preserve that understanding of liberty. Yet the majority invokes our Constitution in the name of a "liberty" that the Framers would not have recognized, to the detriment of the liberty they sought to protect. Along the way, it rejects the idea—captured in our Declaration of Independence—that human dignity is innate and suggests instead that it comes from the Government. This distortion of our Constitution not only ignores the text, it inverts the relationship between the individual and the state in our Republic. I cannot agree with it.

I

The majority's decision today will require States to issue marriage licenses to same-sex couples and to recognize same-sex marriages entered in other States largely based on a constitutional provision guaranteeing "due process" before a person is deprived of his "life, liberty, or property." I have elsewhere explained the dangerous fiction of treating the Due Process Clause as a font of substantive rights. *McDonald* v. *Chicago*, 561 U. S. 742, 811–812 (2010) (THOMAS, J., concurring in part and concurring in judgment). It distorts the constitutional text, which guarantees only whatever "process" is "due" before a person is deprived of life, liberty, and property. U. S. Const., Amdt. 14, §1. Worse, it invites judges to do exactly what the majority has done here—"'roa[m] at large in the constitutional field' guided only by their personal views" as to the "'fundamental rights'" protected by that document. *Planned Parenthood of Southeastern Pa.* v. *Casey*, 505 U. S. 833, 953, 965 (1992) (Rehnquist, C. J., concurring in judgment in part and dissenting in part) (quoting *Griswold* v. *Connecticut*, 381 U. S. 479, 502 (1965) (Harlan, J., concurring in judgment)).

By straying from the text of the Constitution, substantive due process exalts judges at the expense of the People from whom they derive their authority. Petitioners argue that by enshrining the traditional definition of marriage in their State Constitutions through voter-approved amendments, the States have put the issue "beyond the reach of the normal democratic process." Brief for Petitioners in No. 14–562, p. 54. But the result petitioners seek is far less democratic. They ask nine judges on this Court to enshrine their definition of marriage in the Federal Constitution and thus put it beyond the reach of the normal democratic process for the entire Nation. That a "bare majority" of this Court, *ante,* at 25, is able to grant this wish, wiping out with a stroke of the keyboard the results of the political process in over 30 States, based on a provision that guarantees only "due process" is but further evidence of the danger of substantive due process.[1]

II

Even if the doctrine of substantive due process were somehow defensible—it is not—petitioners still would not have a claim. To invoke the protection of the Due Process Clause at all—whether under a theory of "substantive" or "procedural" due process—a party must first identify a deprivation of "life, liberty, or property." The majority claims these state laws deprive petitioners of "liberty," but the concept of "liberty" it conjures up bears no resemblance to any plausible meaning of that word as it is used in the Due Process Clauses.

A

1

As used in the Due Process Clauses, "liberty" most likely refers to "the power of loco-motion, of changing situation, or removing one's person to whatsoever place one's own inclination may direct; without imprisonment or restraint, unless by due course of law." 1 W. Blackstone, Commentaries on the Laws of England 130 (1769) (Blackstone). That definition is drawn from the historical roots of the Clauses and is consistent with our Constitution's text and structure.

Both of the Constitution's Due Process Clauses reach back to Magna Carta. See *Davidson* v. *New Orleans*, 96 U. S. 97, 101–102 (1878). Chapter 39 of the original Magna Carta provided, "No free man shall be taken, imprisoned, disseised, outlawed, banished, or in any way destroyed, nor will We proceed against or prosecute him, except by the lawful judgment of his peers and by the law of the land." Magna Carta, ch. 39, in A. Howard, Magna Carta: Text and Commentary 43 (1964). Although the 1215 version of Magna Carta was in effect for only a few weeks, this provision was later reissued in 1225 with modest changes to its wording as follows: "No freeman shall be taken, or imprisoned, or be disseised of his freehold, or liberties, or free customs, or be outlawed, or exiled, or any otherwise destroyed; nor will we not pass upon him, nor condemn him, but by lawful judgment of his peers or by the law of the land." 1 E. Coke, The Second Part of the Institutes of the Laws of England 45 (1797). In his influential commentary on the provision many years later, Sir Edward Coke interpreted the words "by the law of the land" to mean the same thing as "by due proces of the common law." *Id.,* at 50.

After Magna Carta became subject to renewed interest in the 17th century, see, *e.g., ibid.*, William Blackstone referred to this provision as protecting the "absolute rights of every Englishman." 1 Blackstone 123. And he formulated those absolute rights as "the right of personal security," which included the right to life; "the right of personal liberty"; and "the right of private property." *Id.,* at 125. He defined "the right of personal liberty" as "the power of loco-motion, of changing situation, or removing one's person to whatsoever place one's own inclination may direct; without imprisonment or restraint, unless by due course of law." *Id.*, at 125, 130.[2]

The Framers drew heavily upon Blackstone's formulation, adopting provisions in early State Constitutions that replicated Magna Carta's language, but were modified to refer specifically to "life, liberty, or property."[3] State decisions interpreting these provisions between the founding and the ratification of the Fourteenth Amendment almost uniformly construed the word "liberty" to refer only to freedom from physical restraint. See Warren, The New "Liberty" Under the Fourteenth Amendment, 39 Harv. L. Rev. 431, 441–445 (1926). Even one case that has been identified as a possible exception to that view merely used broad language about liberty in the context of a habeas corpus proceeding—a proceeding classically associated with obtaining freedom from physical restraint. Cf. *id.,* at 444–445.

In enacting the Fifth Amendment's Due Process Clause, the Framers similarly chose to employ the "life, liberty, or property" formulation, though they otherwise deviated substantially from the States' use of Magna Carta's language in the Clause. See Shattuck, The True Meaning of the Term "Liberty" in Those Clauses in the Federal and State Constitutions Which Protect "Life, Liberty, and Property," 4 Harv. L. Rev. 365, 382 (1890). When read in light of the history of that formulation, it is hard to see how the "liberty" protected by the Clause could be interpreted to include anything broader than freedom from physical restraint. That was the consistent usage of the time when "liberty" was paired with "life" and "property." See *id.,* at 375. And that usage avoids rendering superfluous those protections for "life" and "property."

If the Fifth Amendment uses "liberty" in this narrow sense, then the Fourteenth Amendment likely does as well. See *Hurtado* v. *California*, 110 U. S. 516, 534–535 (1884). Indeed, this Court has previously commented, "The conclusion is . . . irresistible, that when the same phrase was employed in the Fourteenth Amendment [as was used in the Fifth Amendment], it was used in the same sense and with no greater extent." *Ibid.* And this Court's earliest Fourteenth Amendment decisions appear to interpret the Clause as using "liberty" to mean freedom from physical restraint. In *Munn* v. *Illinois*, 94 U. S. 113 (1877), for example, the Court recognized the relationship between the two Due Process Clauses and Magna Carta, see *id.,* at 123–124, and implicitly rejected the dissent's argument that "'liberty'" encompassed "something more

. . . than mere freedom from physical restraint or the bounds of a prison," *id.*, at 142 (Field, J., dissenting). That the Court appears to have lost its way in more recent years does not justify deviating from the original meaning of the Clauses.

2

Even assuming that the "liberty" in those Clauses encompasses something more than freedom from physical restraint, it would not include the types of rights claimed by the majority. In the American legal tradition, liberty has long been understood as individual freedom *from* governmental action, not as a right *to* a particular governmental entitlement.

The founding-era understanding of liberty was heavily influenced by John Locke, whose writings "on natural rights and on the social and governmental contract" were cited "[i]n pamphlet after pamphlet" by American writers. B. Bailyn, The Ideological Origins of the American Revolution 27 (1967). Locke described men as existing in a state of nature, possessed of the "perfect freedom to order their actions and dispose of their possessions and persons as they think fit, within the bounds of the law of nature, without asking leave, or depending upon the will of any other man." J. Locke, Second Treatise of Civil Government, §4, p. 4 (J. Gough ed. 1947) (Locke). Because that state of nature left men insecure in their persons and property, they entered civil society, trading a portion of their natural liberty for an increase in their security. See *id.*, §97, at 49. Upon consenting to that order, men obtained civil liberty, or the freedom "to be under no other legislative power but that established by consent in the commonwealth; nor under the dominion of any will or restraint of any law, but what that legislative shall enact according to the trust put in it." *Id.*, §22, at 13.[4]

This philosophy permeated the 18th-century political scene in America. A 1756 editorial in the Boston Gazette, for example, declared that "Liberty in the *State of Nature*" was the "inherent natural Right" "of each Man" "to make a free Use of his Reason and Understanding, and to chuse that Action which he thinks he can give the best Account of," but that, "in Society, every Man parts with a Small Share of his *natural* Liberty, or lodges it in the publick Stock, that he may possess the Remainder without Controul." Boston Gazette and Country Journal, No. 58, May 10, 1756, p. 1. Similar sentiments were expressed in public speeches, sermons, and letters of the time. See 1 C.

Hyneman & D. Lutz, American Political Writing During the Founding Era 1760–1805, pp. 100, 308, 385 (1983).

The founding-era idea of civil liberty as natural liberty constrained by human law necessarily involved only those freedoms that existed *outside of* government. See Hamburger, Natural Rights, Natural Law, and American Constitutions, 102 Yale L. J. 907, 918–919 (1993). As one later commentator observed, "[L]iberty in the eighteenth century was thought of much more in relation to 'negative liberty'; that is, freedom *from*, not freedom *to*, freedom from a number of social and political evils, including arbitrary government power." J. Reid, The Concept of Liberty in the Age of the American Revolution 56 (1988). Or as one scholar put it in 1776, "[T]he common idea of liberty is merely negative, and is only the *absence of restraint.*" R. Hey, Observations on the Nature of Civil Liberty and the Principles of Government §13, p. 8 (1776) (Hey). When the colonists described laws that would infringe their liberties, they discussed laws that would prohibit individuals "from walking in the streets and highways on certain saints days, or from being abroad after a certain time in the evening, or . . . restrain [them] from working up and manufacturing materials of [their] own growth." Downer, A Discourse at the Dedication of the Tree of Liberty, in 1 Hyneman, *supra*, at 101. Each of those examples involved freedoms that existed outside of government.

B

Whether we define "liberty" as locomotion or freedom from governmental action more broadly, petitioners have in no way been deprived of it.

Petitioners cannot claim, under the most plausible definition of "liberty," that they have been imprisoned or physically restrained by the States for participating in same-sex relationships. To the contrary, they have been able to cohabitate and raise their children in peace. They have been able to hold civil marriage ceremonies in States that recognize same-sex marriages and private religious ceremonies in all States. They have been able to travel freely around the country, making their homes where they please. Far from being incarcerated or physically restrained, petitioners have been left alone to order their lives as they see fit.

Nor, under the broader definition, can they claim that the States have restricted their ability to go about their daily lives as they would be able to absent governmental restrictions. Petitioners do not ask this Court to order the States to stop restricting their ability to enter same-sex relationships, to engage in intimate behavior, to make vows to their partners in public ceremonies, to engage in religious wedding ceremonies, to hold themselves out as married, or to raise children. The States have imposed no such restrictions. Nor have the States prevented petitioners from approximating a number of incidents of marriage through private legal means, such as wills, trusts, and powers of attorney.

Instead, the States have refused to grant them governmental entitlements. Petitioners claim that as a matter of "liberty," they are entitled to access privileges and benefits that exist solely *because of* the government. They want, for example, to receive the State's *imprimatur* on their marriages—on state issued marriage licenses, death certificates, or other official forms. And they want to receive various monetary benefits, including reduced inheritance taxes upon the death of a spouse, compensation if a spouse dies as a result of a work-related injury, or loss of consortium damages in tort suits. But receiving governmental recognition and benefits has nothing to do with any understanding of "liberty" that the Framers would have recognized.

To the extent that the Framers would have recognized a natural right to marriage that fell within the broader definition of liberty, it would not have included a right to governmental recognition and benefits. Instead, it would have included a right to engage in the very same activities that petitioners have been left free to engage in—making vows, holding religious ceremonies celebrating those vows, raising children, and otherwise enjoying the society of one's spouse—without governmental interference. At the founding, such conduct was understood to predate government, not to flow from it. As Locke had explained many years earlier, "The first society was between man and wife, which gave beginning to that between parents and children." Locke §77, at 39; see also J. Wilson, Lectures on Law, in 2 Collected Works of James Wilson 1068 (K. Hall and M. Hall eds. 2007) (concluding "that to the institution of marriage the true origin of society must be traced"). Petitioners misunderstand the institution of marriage when they say that it would "mean little" absent governmental recognition. Brief for Petitioners in No. 14– 556, p. 33.

Petitioners' misconception of liberty carries over into their discussion of our precedents identifying a right to marry, not one of which has expanded the concept of "liberty" beyond the concept of negative liberty. Those precedents all involved absolute prohibitions on private actions associated with marriage. *Loving* v. *Virginia*, 388 U. S. 1 (1967), for example, involved a couple who was criminally prosecuted for marrying in the District of Columbia and cohabiting in Virginia, *id.,* at 2–3.[5] They were each sentenced to a year of imprisonment, suspended for a term of 25 years on the condition that they not reenter the Commonwealth together during that time. *Id.,* at 3.[6] In a similar vein, *Zablocki* v. *Redhail*, 434 U. S. 374 (1978), involved a man who was prohibited, on pain of criminal penalty, from "marry[ing] in Wisconsin or elsewhere" because of his outstanding child-support obligations, *id.,* at 387; see *id.,* at 377–378. And *Turner* v. *Safley*, 482 U. S. 78 (1987), involved state inmates who were prohibited from entering marriages without the permission of the superintendent of the prison, permission that could not be granted absent compelling reasons, *id.,* at 82. In *none* of those cases were individuals denied solely governmental recognition and benefits associated with marriage.

In a concession to petitioners' misconception of liberty, the majority characterizes petitioners' suit as a quest to "find . . . liberty by marrying someone of the same sex and having their marriages deemed lawful on the same terms and conditions as marriages between persons of the opposite sex." *Ante,* at 2. But "liberty" is not lost, nor can it be found in the way petitioners seek. As a philosophical matter, liberty is only freedom from governmental action, not an entitlement to governmental benefits. And as a constitutional matter, it is likely even narrower than that, encompassing only freedom from physical restraint and imprisonment. The majority's "better informed understanding of how constitutional imperatives define . . . liberty," *ante,* at 19,—better informed, we must assume, than that of the people who ratified the Fourteenth Amendment—runs headlong into the reality that our Constitution is a "collection of 'Thou shalt nots,'" *Reid* v. *Covert*, 354 U. S. 1, 9 (1957) (plurality opinion), not "Thou shalt provides."

III

The majority's inversion of the original meaning of liberty will likely cause collateral damage to other aspects of our constitutional order that protect liberty.

A

The majority apparently disregards the political process as a protection for liberty. Although men, in forming a civil society, "give up all the power necessary to the ends for which they unite into society, to the majority of the community," Locke §99, at 49, they reserve the authority to exercise natural liberty within the bounds of laws established by that society, *id.,* §22, at 13; see also Hey §§52, 54, at 30–32. To protect that liberty from arbitrary interference, they establish a process by which that society can adopt and enforce its laws. In our country, that process is primarily representative government at the state level, with the Federal Constitution serving as a backstop for that process. As a general matter, when the States act through their representative governments or by popular vote, the liberty of their residents is fully vindicated. This is no less true when some residents disagree with the result; indeed, it seems difficult to imagine *any* law on which all residents of a State would agree. See Locke §98, at 49 (suggesting that society would cease to function if it required unanimous consent to laws). What matters is that the process established by those who created the society has been honored.

That process has been honored here. The definition of marriage has been the subject of heated debate in the States. Legislatures have repeatedly taken up the matter on behalf of the People, and 35 States have put the question to the People themselves. In 32 of those 35 States, the People have opted to retain the traditional definition of marriage. Brief for Respondents in No. 14–571, pp. 1a– 7a. That petitioners disagree with the result of that process does not make it any less legitimate. Their civil liberty has been vindicated.

B

Aside from undermining the political processes that protect our liberty, the majority's decision threatens the religious liberty our Nation has long sought to protect.

The history of religious liberty in our country is familiar: Many of the earliest immigrants to America came seeking freedom to practice their religion without restraint. See McConnell, The Origins and Historical Understanding of Free Exercise of Religion, 103 Harv. L. Rev. 1409, 1422– 1425 (1990). When they arrived, they created their own havens for religious practice. *Ibid.* Many of these havens were initially homogenous communities with established religions. *Ibid.* By the 1780's, however, "America was in the wake of a great religious revival" marked by a move toward free exercise of religion. *Id.,* at 1437. Every State save Connecticut adopted protections for religious freedom in their State Constitutions by 1789, *id.,* at 1455, and, of course, the First Amendment enshrined protection for the free exercise of religion in the U. S. Constitution. But that protection was far from the last word on religious liberty in this country, as the Federal Government and the States have reaffirmed their commitment to religious liberty by codifying protections for religious practice. See, *e.g.,* Religious Freedom Restoration Act of 1993, 107 Stat. 1488, 42 U. S. C. §2000bb *et seq.*; Conn. Gen. Stat. §52–571b (2015).

Numerous *amici*—even some not supporting the States—have cautioned the Court that its decision here will "have unavoidable and wide-ranging implications for religious liberty." Brief for General Conference of Seventh-Day Adventists et al. as *Amici Curiae* 5. In our society, marriage is not simply a governmental institution; it is a religious institution as well. *Id.,* at 7. Today's decision might change the former, but it cannot change the latter. It appears all but inevitable that the two will come into conflict, particularly as individuals and churches are confronted with demands to participate in and endorse civil marriages between same-sex couples.

The majority appears unmoved by that inevitability. It makes only a weak gesture toward religious liberty in a single paragraph, *ante,* at 27. And even that gesture indicates a misunderstanding of religious liberty in our Nation's tradition. Religious liberty is about more than just the protection for "religious organizations and persons . . . as they seek to teach the principles that are so fulfilling and so central to their lives and faiths." *Ibid.* Religious liberty is about freedom of action in matters of religion generally, and the scope of that liberty is directly correlated to the civil restraints placed upon religious practice.[7]

Although our Constitution provides some protection against such governmental restrictions on religious practices, the People have long elected to afford broader protections than this Court's constitutional precedents mandate. Had the majority allowed the definition of marriage to be left to the political process—as the Constitution requires—the People could have considered the religious liberty implications of deviating from the traditional definition as part of their deliberative process. Instead, the majority's decision short-circuits that process, with potentially ruinous consequences for religious liberty.

IV

Perhaps recognizing that these cases do not actually involve liberty as it has been understood, the majority goes to great lengths to assert that its decision will advance the "dignity" of same-sex couples. *Ante,* at 3, 13, 26,

28.[8] The flaw in that reasoning, of course, is that the Constitution contains no "dignity" Clause, and even if it did, the government would be incapable of bestowing dignity.

Human dignity has long been understood in this country to be innate. When the Framers proclaimed in the Declaration of Independence that "all men are created equal" and "endowed by their Creator with certain unalienable Rights," they referred to a vision of mankind in which all humans are created in the image of God and therefore of inherent worth. That vision is the foundation upon which this Nation was built.

The corollary of that principle is that human dignity cannot be taken away by the government. Slaves did not lose their dignity (any more than they lost their humanity) because the government allowed them to be enslaved. Those held in internment camps did not lose their dignity because the government confined them. And those denied governmental benefits certainly do not lose their dignity because the government denies them those benefits. The government cannot bestow dignity, and it cannot take it away.

The majority's musings are thus deeply misguided, but at least those musings can have no effect on the dignity of the persons the majority demeans. Its mischaracterization of the arguments presented by the States and their *amici* can have no effect on the dignity of those litigants. Its rejection of laws preserving the traditional definition of marriage can have no effect on the dignity of the people who voted for them. Its invalidation of those laws can have no effect on the dignity of the people who continue to adhere to the traditional definition of marriage. And its disdain for the understandings of liberty and dignity upon which this Nation was founded can have no effect on the dignity of Americans who continue to believe in them.

* * *

Our Constitution—like the Declaration of Independence before it—was predicated on a simple truth: One's liberty, not to mention one's dignity, was something to be shielded from—not provided by—the State. Today's decision casts that truth aside. In its haste to reach a desired result, the majority misapplies a clause focused on "due process" to afford substantive rights, disregards the most plausible understanding of the "liberty" protected by that clause, and distorts the principles on which this Nation was founded. Its decision will have inestimable consequences for our Constitution and our society. I respectfully dissent.

ALITO, J., DISSENTING

SUPREME COURT OF THE UNITED STATES
Nos. 14–556, 14-562, 14-571 and 14–574
JAMES OBERGEFELL, ET AL., PETITIONERS
14–556 *v.*
RICHARD HODGES, DIRECTOR, OHIO DEPARTMENT OF HEALTH, ET AL.;
VALERIA TANCO, ET AL., PETITIONERS
14–562 *v.*
BILL HASLAM, GOVERNOR OF TENNESSEE, ET AL.;
APRIL DEBOER, ET AL., PETITIONERS
14–571 *v.*
RICK SNYDER, GOVERNOR OF MICHIGAN, ET AL.; AND
GREGORY BOURKE, ET AL., PETITIONERS
14–574 *v.*
STEVE BESHEAR, GOVERNOR OF KENTUCKY
ON WRITS OF CERTIORARI TO THE UNITED STATES COURT OF APPEALS FOR THE SIXTH CIRCUIT
[June 26, 2015]

JUSTICE ALITO, with whom JUSTICE SCALIA and JUSTICE THOMAS join, dissenting.

Until the federal courts intervened, the American people were engaged in a debate about whether their States should recognize same-sex marriage.[1] The question in these cases, however, is not what States *should* do about same-sex marriage but whether the Constitution answers that question for them. It does not. The Constitution leaves that question to be decided by the people of each State.

I

The Constitution says nothing about a right to same-sex marriage, but the Court holds that the term "liberty" in the Due Process Clause of the Fourteenth

Amendment encompasses this right. Our Nation was founded upon the principle that every person has the unalienable right to liberty, but liberty is a term of many meanings. For classical liberals, it may include economic rights now limited by government regulation. For social democrats, it may include the right to a variety of government benefits. For today's majority, it has a distinctively postmodern meaning.

To prevent five unelected Justices from imposing their personal vision of liberty upon the American people, the Court has held that "liberty" under the Due Process Clause should be understood to protect only those rights that are "'deeply rooted in this Nation's history and tradition.'" *Washington* v. *Glucksberg*, 521 U. S. 701, 720–721 (1997). And it is beyond dispute that the right to same-sex marriage is not among those rights. See *United States* v. *Windsor*, 570 U. S. ___, ___ (2013) (ALITO, J., dissenting) (slip op., at 7). Indeed:

> "In this country, no State permitted same-sex marriage until the Massachusetts Supreme Judicial Court held in 2003 that limiting marriage to opposite-sex couples violated the State Constitution. See *Goodridge* v. *Department of Public Health*, 440 Mass.
>
> 309, 798 N. E. 2d 941. Nor is the right to same-sex marriage deeply rooted in the traditions of other nations. No country allowed same-sex couples to marry until the Netherlands did so in 2000.
>
> "What [those arguing in favor of a constitutional right to same sex marriage] seek, therefore, is not the protection of a deeply rooted right but the recognition of a very new right, and they seek this innovation not from a legislative body elected by the people, but from unelected judges. Faced with such a request, judges have cause for both caution and humility." *Id.,* at ___ (slip op., at 7–8) (footnote omitted).

For today's majority, it does not matter that the right to same-sex marriage lacks deep roots or even that it is contrary to long-established tradition. The Justices in the majority claim the authority to confer constitutional protection upon that right simply because they believe that it is fundamental.

II

Attempting to circumvent the problem presented by the newness of the right found in these cases, the majority claims that the issue is the right to equal treatment. Noting that marriage is a fundamental right, the majority argues that a State has no valid reason for denying that right to same-sex couples. This reasoning is dependent upon a particular understanding of the purpose of civil marriage. Although the Court expresses the point in loftier terms, its argument is that the fundamental purpose of marriage is to promote the well-being of those who choose to marry. Marriage provides emotional fulfillment and the promise of support in times of need. And by benefiting persons who choose to wed, marriage indirectly benefits society because persons who live in stable, fulfilling, and supportive relationships make better citizens. It is for these reasons, the argument goes, that States encourage and formalize marriage, confer special benefits on married persons, and also impose some special obligations. This understanding of the States' reasons for recognizing marriage enables the majority to argue that same-sex marriage serves the States' objectives in the same way as opposite-sex marriage.

This understanding of marriage, which focuses almost entirely on the happiness of persons who choose to marry, is shared by many people today, but it is not the traditional one. For millennia, marriage was inextricably linked to the one thing that only an opposite-sex couple can do: procreate.

Adherents to different schools of philosophy use different terms to explain why society should formalize marriage and attach special benefits and obligations to persons who marry. Here, the States defending their adherence to the traditional understanding of marriage have explained their position using the pragmatic vocabulary that characterizes most American political discourse. Their basic argument is that States formalize and promote marriage, unlike other fulfilling human relationships, in order to encourage potentially procreative conduct to take place within a lasting unit that has long been thought to provide the best atmosphere for raising children. They thus argue that there are reasonable secular grounds for restricting marriage to opposite-sex couples.

If this traditional understanding of the purpose of marriage does not ring true to all ears today, that is probably because the tie between marriage and procreation has frayed. Today, for instance, more than 40% of all children in this country are born to unmarried women.[2] This development undoubtedly is both a cause and a result of changes in our society's understanding of marriage.

While, for many, the attributes of marriage in 21st-century America have changed, those States that do not want to recognize same-sex marriage have not yet given up on the traditional understanding. They worry that by officially abandoning the older understanding, they may contribute to marriage's further decay. It is far beyond the outer reaches of this Court's authority to say that a

State may not adhere to the understanding of marriage that has long prevailed, not just in this country and others with similar cultural roots, but also in a great variety of countries and cultures all around the globe.

As I wrote in *Windsor*:

> "The family is an ancient and universal human institution. Family structure reflects the characteristics of a civilization, and changes in family structure and in the popular understanding of marriage and the family can have profound effects. Past changes in the understanding of marriage—for example, the gradual ascendance of the idea that romantic love is a prerequisite to marriage—have had far-reaching consequences. But the process by which such consequences come about is complex, involving the interaction of numerous factors, and tends to occur over an extended period of time.
>
> "We can expect something similar to take place if same-sex marriage becomes widely accepted. The long-term consequences of this change are not now known and are unlikely to be ascertainable for some time to come. There are those who think that allowing same-sex marriage will seriously undermine the institution of marriage. Others think that recogni- tion of same-sex marriage will fortify a now-shaky institution.
>
> "At present, no one—including social scientists, philosophers, and historians—can predict with any certainty what the long-term ramifications of widespread acceptance of same-sex marriage will be. And judges are certainly not equipped to make such an assessment. The Members of this Court have the authority and the responsibility to interpret and apply the Constitution.
>
> Thus, if the Constitution contained a provision guaranteeing the right to marry a person of the same sex, it would be our duty to enforce that right. But the Constitution simply does not speak to the issue of same-sex marriage. In our system of government, ultimate sovereignty rests with the people, and the people have the right to control their own destiny. Any change on a question so fundamental should be made by the people through their elected officials." 570 U. S., at ___ (dissenting opinion) (slip op., at 8–10) (citations and footnotes omitted).

III

Today's decision usurps the constitutional right of the people to decide whether to keep or alter the traditional understanding of marriage. The decision will also have other important consequences.

It will be used to vilify Americans who are unwilling to assent to the new orthodoxy. In the course of its opinion, the majority compares traditional marriage laws to laws that denied equal treatment for African-Americans and women. *E.g.*, *ante*, at 11–13. The implications of this analogy will be exploited by those who are determined to stamp out every vestige of dissent.

Perhaps recognizing how its reasoning may be used, the majority attempts, toward the end of its opinion, to reassure those who oppose same-sex marriage that their rights of conscience will be protected. *Ante*, at 26–27. We will soon see whether this proves to be true. I assume that those who cling to old beliefs will be able to whisper their thoughts in the recesses of their homes, but if they repeat those views in public, they will risk being labeled as bigots and treated as such by governments, employers, and schools.

The system of federalism established by our Constitution provides a way for people with different beliefs to live together in a single nation. If the issue of same-sex marriage had been left to the people of the States, it is likely that some States would recognize same-sex marriage and others would not. It is also possible that some States would tie recognition to protection for conscience rights.

The majority today makes that impossible. By imposing its own views on the entire country, the majority facilitates the marginalization of the many Americans who have traditional ideas. Recalling the harsh treatment of gays and lesbians in the past, some may think that turn- about is fair play. But if that sentiment prevails, the Na- tion will experience bitter and lasting wounds.

Today's decision will also have a fundamental effect on this Court and its ability to uphold the rule of law. If a bare majority of Justices can invent a new right and impose that right on the rest of the country, the only real limit on what future majorities will be able to do is their own sense of what those with political power and cultural influence are willing to tolerate. Even enthusiastic supporters of same-sex marriage should worry about the scope of the power that today's majority claims.

Today's decision shows that decades of attempts to restrain this Court's abuse of its authority have failed. A lesson that some will take from today's decision is that preaching about the proper method of interpreting the Constitution or the virtues of judicial self-restraint and humility cannot compete with the temptation to achieve what is viewed as a noble end by any practicable means. I do not doubt that my colleagues in the majority sincerely see in the Constitution a vision of liberty that happens to coincide with their own.

But this sincerity is cause for concern, not comfort. What it evidences is the deep and perhaps irremediable corruption of our legal culture's conception of constitutional interpretation.

Most Americans—understandably—will cheer or lament today's decision because of their views on the issue of same-sex marriage. But all Americans, whatever their thinking on that issue, should worry about what the majority's claim of power portends.

End Notes for Scalia, J., Dissenting

[1] Brief for Respondents in No. 14–571, p. 14.

[2] Accord, *Schuette* v. *BAMN*, 572 U. S. ___, ___–___ (2014) (plurality opinion) (slip op., at 15–17).

[3] U. S. Const., Art. I, §10.

[4] Art. IV, §1.

[5] Amdt. 1.

[6] *Ibid.*

[7] Amdt. 2.

[8] Amdt. 4.

[9] Amdt. 10.

[10] *United States* v. *Windsor*, 570 U. S. ___, ___ (2013) (slip op., at 16) (internal quotation marks and citation omitted).

[11] *Id.*, at ___ (slip op., at 17).

[12] See *Town of Greece* v. *Galloway*, 572 U. S. ___, ___–___ (2014) (slip op., at 7–8).

[13] *Ante*, at 10.

[14] *Ante*, at 11.

[15] *Ibid.*

[16] *Ante*, at 10–11.

[17] *Ante*, at 12–18.

[18] The predominant attitude of tall-building lawyers with respect to the questions presented in these cases is suggested by the fact that the American Bar Association deemed it in accord with the wishes of its members to file a brief in support of the petitioners. See Brief for American Bar Association as *Amicus Curiae* in Nos. 14–571 and 14– 574, pp. 1–5.

[19] See Pew Research Center, America's Changing Religious Landscape 4 (May 12, 2015).

[20] *Goodridge* v. *Department of Public Health*, 440 Mass. 309, 798 N. E. 2d 941 (2003).

[21] *Windsor*, 570 U. S., at ___ (ALITO, J., dissenting) (slip op., at 7).

[22] If, even as the price to be paid for a fifth vote, I ever joined an opinion for the Court that began: "The Constitution promises liberty to all within its reach, a liberty that includes certain specific rights that allow persons, within a lawful realm, to define and express their identity," I would hide my head in a bag. The Supreme Court of the United States has descended from the disciplined legal reasoning of John Marshall and Joseph Story to the mystical aphorisms of the fortune cookie.

[23] *Ante*, at 13.

[24] *Ante*, at 19.

[25] *Ibid.*

[26] The Federalist No. 78, pp. 522, 523 (J. Cooke ed. 1961) (A. Hamilton).

End Notes for Thomas, J., Dissenting

[1] The majority states that the right it believes is "part of the liberty promised by the Fourteenth Amendment is derived, too, from that Amendment's guarantee of the equal protection of the laws." *Ante,* at 19. Despite the "synergy" it finds "between th[ese] two protections," *ante*, at 20, the majority clearly uses equal protection only to shore up its substantive due process analysis, an analysis both based on an imaginary constitutional protection and revisionist view of our history and tradition.

[2] The seeds of this articulation can also be found in Henry Care's influential treatise, English Liberties. First published in America in 1721, it described the "three things, which the Law of *England* . . . principally regards and taketh Care of," as "*Life*, *Liberty* and *Estate*," and described habeas corpus as the means by which one could procure one's "Liberty" from imprisonment. The Habeas Corpus Act, comment., in English Liberties, or the Free-born Subject's Inheritance 185 (H. Care comp. 5th ed. 1721). Though he used the word "Liberties" by itself more broadly, see, *e.g., id.,* at 7, 34, 56, 58, 60, he used "Liberty" in a narrow sense when placed alongside the words "Life" or "Estate," see, *e.g., id.,* at 185, 200.

[3] Maryland, North Carolina, and South Carolina adopted the phrase "life, liberty, or property" in provisions otherwise tracking Magna Carta: "That no freeman ought to be taken, or imprisoned, or disseized of his freehold, liberties, or privileges, or outlawed, or exiled, or in any manner destroyed, or deprived of his life, liberty, or property, but by the judgment of his peers, or by the law of the land." Md. Const., Declaration of Rights, Art. XXI (1776), in 3 Federal and State Constitutions, Colonial Charters, and Other Organic Laws 1688 (F. Thorpe ed. 1909); see also S. C. Const., Art. XLI (1778), in 6 *id.,* at 3257; N. C. Const., Declaration of Rights, Art. XII (1776), in 5 *id.,* at 2788. Massachusetts and New Hampshire did the same, albeit with some alterations to Magna Carta's framework: "[N]o subject shall be arrested, imprisoned, despoiled, or deprived of his property, immunities, or privileges, put out of the protection of the law, exiled, or deprived of his life, liberty, or estate, but by the judgment of his peers, or the law of the land." Mass. Const., pt. I, Art. XII (1780), in 3 *id.,* at 1891; see also N. H. Const., pt. I, Art. XV (1784), in 4 *id.,* at 2455.

[4] Locke's theories heavily influenced other prominent writers of the 17th and 18th centuries. Blackstone, for one, agreed that "natural liberty consists properly in a power of acting as one thinks fit, without any restraint or control, unless by the law of nature" and described civil liberty as that "which leaves the subject entire master of his own conduct," except as "restrained by human laws." 1 Blackstone 121–122. And in a "treatise routinely cited by the Founders," *Zivotofsky* v. *Kerry*, *ante,* at 5 (THOMAS, J., concurring in judgment in part and dissenting in part), Thomas Rutherforth wrote, "By liberty we mean the power, which a man has to act as he thinks fit, where no law restrains him; it may therefore be called a mans right over his own actions." 1 T. Rutherforth, Institutes of Natural Law 146 (1754). Rutherforth explained that "[t]he only restraint, which a mans right over his own actions is originally under, is the obligation of governing himself by the law of nature, and the law of God," and that "[w]hatever right those of our own species may have . . . to restrain [those actions] within certain bounds, beyond what the law of nature has prescribed, arises from some after-act of our own, from some consent either express or tacit, by which we have

alienated our liberty, or transferred the right of directing our actions from ourselves to them." *Id.*, at 147–148.

[5] The suggestion of petitioners and their *amici* that antimiscegenation laws are akin to laws defining marriage as between one man and one woman is both offensive and inaccurate. "America's earliest laws against interracial sex and marriage were spawned by slavery." P. Pascoe, What Comes Naturally: Miscegenation Law and the Making of Race in America 19 (2009). For instance, Maryland's 1664 law prohibiting marriages between " 'freeborne English women' " and " 'Negro Sla[v]es' " was passed as part of the very act that authorized lifelong slavery in the colony. *Id.*, at 19–20. Virginia's antimiscegenation laws likewise were passed in a 1691 resolution entitled "An act for suppressing outlying Slaves." Act of Apr. 1691, Ch. XVI, 3 Va. Stat. 86 (W. Hening ed. 1823) (reprint 1969) (italics deleted). "It was not until the Civil War threw the future of slavery into doubt that lawyers, legislators, and judges began to develop the elaborate justifications that signified the emergence of miscegenation law and made restrictions on interracial marriage the foundation of post-Civil War white supremacy." Pascoe, *supra*, at 27–28.

Laws defining marriage as between one man and one woman do not share this sordid history. The traditional definition of marriage has prevailed in every society that has recognized marriage throughout history. Brief for Scholars of History and Related Disciplines as *Amici Curiae* 1. It arose not out of a desire to shore up an invidious institution like slavery, but out of a desire "to increase the likelihood that children will be born and raised in stable and enduring family units by both the mothers and the fathers who brought them into this world." *Id.*, at 8. And it has existed in civilizations containing all manner of views on homosexuality. See Brief for Ryan T. Anderson as *Amicus Curiae* 11–12 (explaining that several famous ancient Greeks wrote approvingly of the traditional definition of marriage, though same-sex sexual relations were common in Greece at the time).

[6] The prohibition extended so far as to forbid even religious ceremonies, thus raising a serious question under the First Amendment's Free Exercise Clause, as at least one *amicus* brief at the time pointed out. Brief for John J. Russell et al. as *Amici Curiae* in *Loving* v. *Virginia*, O.T. 1966, No. 395, pp. 12–16.

[7] Concerns about threats to religious liberty in this context are not unfounded. During the hey-day of antimiscegenation laws in this country, for instance, Virginia imposed criminal penalties on ministers who performed marriage in violation of those laws, though their religions would have permitted them to perform such ceremonies. Va. Code Ann. §20–60 (1960).

[8] The majority also suggests that marriage confers "nobility" on individuals. *Ante,* at 3. I am unsure what that means. People may choose to marry or not to marry. The decision to do so does not make one person more "noble" than another. And the suggestion that Americans who choose not to marry are inferior to those who decide to enter such relationships is specious.

End Notes for Alito, J., Dissenting

[1] I use the phrase "recognize marriage" as shorthand for issuing marriage licenses and conferring those special benefits and obligations provided under state law for married persons.

[2] See, *e.g.,* Dept. of Health and Human Services, Centers for Disease Control and Prevention, National Center for Health Statistics, D. Martin, B. Hamilton, M. Osterman, S. Curtin, & T.

Matthews, Births: Final Data for 2013, 64 National Vital Statistics Reports, No. 1, p. 2 (Jan. 15, 2015), online at http://www.cdc.gov/nchs/data/nvsr/nvsr64/nvsr64_01.pdf (all Internet materials as visited June 24, 2015, and available in Clerk of Court's case file); cf. Dept. of Health and Human Services, Centers for Disease Control and Prevention, National Center for Health Statistics (NCHS), S. Ventura, Changing Patterns of Non-martial Childbearing in the United States, NCHS Data Brief, No. 18 (May 2009), online at http://www.cdc.gov/nchs/data/databrief/db18.pdf.

INDEX

D

E

J

L

M

N

O

P

Q

R

S

T

U

V